# The Woman I Love

## Surviving, Healing and Thriving After a Childhood of Sexual, Emotional, and Physical Abuse

Becky Norwood

Publisher: MBK Enterprises, LLC
Publication Date: 2016
©2016 by Becky B. Norwood. All Rights Reserved
Printed in USA
ISBN: ISBN-10:0-9971687-2-2
    ISBN-13:978-0-9971687-2-3
Library of Congress Control Number: 2016910568
Edited by: Jay Polmar   Speed Read America
Design, Layout and Graphics by: Becky Norwood
Cover Design by: Angie Ayala
Foreword by: Susan Ferreira

This book is based on the real live personal experience and opinions of the author. Please note that names and places have been changed to protect the identity of those involved.  The author will not be held liable or responsible to any person or entity with respect to alleged damages caused directly or indirectly by the information within this book.

Contact the Author:  Becky Norwood  thewomaniloveisme@gmail.com

# *Dedication*

This book is dedicated to all victims of abuse...no matter the type of abuse.

Regardless of where you are right now on your path to recovery and healing, my deepest desire is to shine light on the power of forgiveness and loving yourself, first and foremost.

I pray that you will find comfort, hope and healing, to the point that you too can stand up, and tell your own story with authenticity and grace. My desire is that together, we can be the change we need to see in the world.

# Foreword

Written by Susan Ferreira

How fortunate am I never to have suffered sexual abuse and the long lasting pain it leaves within the victims' souls, for the remainder of their lives.

Sexual abuse stays with you forever, even if you have come to terms with it, have bravely transformed your life and created good relationships and families.

Sexual abuse never goes away.

Even after over 40 years as an anesthesiologist, I knew little about sexual abuse and its prevalence. My experience was limited to providing anesthesia for young children, usually girls, for their post-rape examinations, for both legal and medical reasons. In the Operating Rooms, at these times, there was a sad silence, as we all felt sick at the violation of a young child. Who could do such a thing, we would murmur. What is in the mind of such a monster?

Now, later in my life, after retiring from medicine and becoming an entrepreneur for my second act, I am helping women build their businesses and move online and one of my programs is helping women tell their story.

Knowing who you are and understanding your story is of great value to anyone in business, as it gives you your "Why", the reason you do what you do.

Within a few months after I began helping women tell their stories, I found myself surrounded by five new friends, women for whom I had gained a great respect - wonderful warm, strong and giving women - who had built beautiful lives, but whom I discovered to my sadness, all had a history of sexual abuse, as children.

Some had already "come out" with their stories, others were still struggling.

Sexual abuse comes in many forms - abuse by the Catholic Clergy and other institutions, abuse by unknown sexual predators, college rape and incest, sexual abuse by a family member or family members.

Abuse by the Catholic Clergy has been blown wide open in the past few years, though the Catholic Church's response has hardly been accepting or proactive to prevent further abuse.

Abuse by sexual predators is the least common of these abuses, but it leaves scars of fear forever.

College Rape has been blown open recently, following the publicity surrounding the culture of campus rape in Missoula, Montana. The chances are the same happens on all campuses, the University of Montana happened to be the first, where a strong woman reported her rape and wouldn't back down. Understandably, many do, for they are portrayed as being at fault, whilst as in a recent case, the perpetrator's crime was dismissed by his father as "20 minutes of action."

But incest is the last taboo. Incest is still "not talked about", because incest is the ultimate in betrayal. For a victim of incest, the insults and abuse are inflicted within the area, where they are meant to be safe and surrounded by love. A young child subjected to the trauma of repeated rape by a family member, has nowhere to go, nowhere to hide and they know the rape will be repeated time and again.

In most cases, the family is in denial; often the mother does nothing to save her child, for she too lives in fear. This denial continues for decades and my friends, who were the victims of incest, all struggled with going public with their stories, for fear of the repercussions within the family and the rejection they, the victim, not the perpetrator, would face.

I met Becky Norwood about four years ago, at an event in San Diego, where we were both looking to build a new business, using the power of the web and web marketing. Immediately, we felt a bond. I instantly admired this strong, intelligent, creative woman and although we live a thousand miles apart, we kept in touch and saw each other a couple of times a year in San Diego, where we continued to deepen our friendship.

Slowly, I learned a little more about Becky. I learned she had left her first marriage, when her two daughters were very young and that she had worked hard building several businesses and home schooling her girls. Little did I know then, she was schooling herself at the same time to make up for a childhood of disruption and a lack of education.

I knew she adored her daughters and had recently remarried to Mark, whom she describes as the kindest and most supportive man in the world and I would have to agree with her.

Somehow, I knew there was more, but also knew not to ask.

One day, about a year ago, Becky mentioned she had bought her perfect website name four years earlier. It was "The Woman I Love" but she couldn't bring herself to tell her story. Becky bought the website name in her fifty-fifth year. She had carried her story in her soul for half a century and still remained silent, not wanting to face the pain of her history.

This year, Becky's sixtieth year, the dam broke. One Sunday this past spring, we spent the day together in La Jolla, California. We had a large breakfast and then we walked and walked and talked. Slowly, Becky told me her story. This is a story not only of repeated sexual abuse from her father, but one of physical, religious and emotional abuse.

One comment Becky made hurt my heart and I felt I had been pierced with an arrow. She said she had never felt joy. She always felt outside of any laughter and could not join the merriment of the group and this from this beautiful, strong, gentle survivor, who had raised her kids on her own and built several businesses. She also revealed she didn't feel she had found her passion in life and wasn't sure where to go next.

By the end of our long walk, Becky decided to write her story, as we both knew the act of writing down your story brings an emotional release and relief.

Here a few months later, we have Becky's story. It is not one of "Poor Me" but it is her story and telling it has brought her a release and has awakened her passion to help others through telling their stories, by providing a safe place for those who have also suffered from incestual abuse to find relief and release by writing their stories, anonymously, if wished.

She is also building a community committed to publicizing the insult and terrible lasting effects of incestual rape.

This week, Becky and I were on a video chat where I was overwhelmed by the transformation and radiance of this wonderful woman. Tears came to my eyes, as they are doing now writing these words, when Becky told me she has never felt happier and feels a great joy in her life.

If you have a story of abuse, incestual or otherwise, within you, go to **www.TheWomanILove.com** and accept Becky's invitation to tell your story and join her community of women who have bravely confronted the demons of their past and are determined that others will not suffer similar abuse.

# Acknowledgements

his book would not be complete without the salute of honor that I hold in my heart for you my darling and amazing husband, Mark. Honey, your love, wisdom and heart have given me the strength to heal and to become whole. You have stayed by my side and loved me through it all! You've taken my children under wing, without being demanding or in expectation of more than they were willing to give in return. You watch over me with tenderness and care, which endears me to you even more. I adore you!

To my stepdad Mike. You have been kind, patient and loving to my Mom, helping her to also heal. You've also put up with the this family in both the early and the continued stages of our recovery. Ever the gentleman, I know there has been many times you've had to hold both your thoughts and your tongue. Thank you!

To my Mom. You have had the courage to grow and heal. You prove that no matter our age, we can all seek to be the very best we can be. Given a new set of surroundings, love and support, is proof positive that change is possible. You too have come to the understanding that forgiving is something we do for ourselves and loving yourself is the kindest way to heal. I am proud of you!

To my daughter Jenny. You are the most amazing young woman I have ever known. You have heart, wisdom beyond your years, an incredible understanding of the nature of people and a kindness that will forever make me proud. You know how to be a great friend to your own friends and are always so giving. You will always be my Egyptian Goddess.

To Lydia, my Beautiful Princess, thank you for bringing my awesome grandson into this world and allowing me to be so much a part of his life. He is my world and my sunshine. My prayer is that you will always remember that the power of love and forgiveness is the key to happiness. Never forget how much your family loves you. Never forget to love YOU first. I know you are strong and smart and will make the best decisions for you and your little man.

To my Auntie Jenn. As a child I was always told that I was so much like you...and indeed that has proven to be the case. While we missed some 40+ years of being a part of each others lives, I am forever grateful to the loving friendship we now share. Our hours of conversation and working together on projects has been delightful and I treasure every moment.

To my brother: My prayer for you is that you find peace in your heart and always strive to live in accord with the promptings your heart gives you. You and your family have lost so much. I admire that you are the man that you are in spite of the deep personal pain of losing two children. You are a man that gives and gives...remember that giving love and forgiveness to yourself always is our truest healer.

To my "bonus" family of kids and grandkids, thank you for loving and accepting me into your lives. You all have added so much richness to my life and I love you.

To Fred and Carol C. who were my angels of love as a child and who remain friends to this day. You always put a smile on my face no matter how tough times were. You both are the reason I am alive today.

To my cherished forever friend Bob K. who gave me hope, taught me friendship, unconditional love and treated my daughters to many wonderful first time special memories. You will forever be the first man to ever show my daughters how a father should be.

And now to all of my angels. Many of you, I will never know your names, yet you've made such an impact on my life simply by being you. From that first couple who brought me home that evening when I stood on a Los Angeles street corner so very long ago, to the author whose book I picked up in old San Diego recently...and all in between.

To my friends and mentors, who have so patiently stood by my side. You've offered your wisdom, shared your stories and loved me in spite and despite it all. You've watched me learn to laugh, love and trust, fall down, cry, get back up and continue on. To Sue F., Pat C., Krista L, Traci K., Valerie K., Paul and Melinda B., Erica Y., Judy C., Miguel de J., Valerie K., D'Vorah L., Bree W., and SO many more that time and space won't permit me to acknowledge. Thank you with all the gratefulness of my heart.

To all of those whose books I have read, who have had the courage to tell their stories long before I have mustered the courage to tell my own. It is my desire that our collective stories will impact the consciousness of our world, with the result bringing awareness that leads to the change we so need in this world.

# Table of Contents

*Chapter 1*

# "I Do Not Owe My Past a Place in My Future"

Sitting in the audience of a recent seminar, I heard the words above and it hit me like thunder.

Then, while reading the book, Rising Strong: The Reckoning, The Rumble and The Revolution by Brené Brown, I found a quote that resonated well.

> *"The irony is that we attempt to disown our difficult stories to appear more whole or more acceptable. But our wholeness, even our wholeheartedness actually depends on the integration of all of our experiences, including the falls."*

I've known it was time to write this book for five long years. However, to share the breadth and scope of this story, I would have to love and accept myself, for the role I played and for my own failures as well.

*I would have to bare my soul for the world to see.*

This is a true story meant to serve as a connector. As humans, we relish stories and well told stories can have a huge impact for transformational change in the lives of the readers.

Me? I will pick up a book and read it cover to cover if it is a story of someone's life. I can get totally immersed in the storyline, closely following the events, good or bad that made them who they are today.

I am fully aware that none of us can exist in a vacuum, and as such we don't complete our lives on this earth without some sort of life changing event. Something that happened that has forced us to make some kind of serious decision regarding what we truly want in our lives.

We all are a constantly unfolding story. We are the hero in a novel that no one else can write. For most of us, our journey in this life is to find love, balance and peace. The road we travel carves the way for life lessons that fine tune us to have the strength, the power, and the where-with-all to move through our challenges.

Ultimately, we have decisions to make. Sometimes we fail miserably and fall flat. Other times we can pass with flying colors. But it always comes down to the choices we make. Depending on the scope of the situation, it may take many years to rise above the circumstances and succeed.

For me…It did take years…many years. And because it took *YEARS*, I've struggled with bouts of depression, feelings of inadequacy and shame. The "if only I's…" only serve as a plague…because, truly the past is OVER and cannot be changed and *THIS is the ONLY* moment I can experience.

The inability to simply have fun with life, to even be able to let loose and wholeheartedly laugh has plagued me since early childhood.

While today, I still tend to be very serious, I have learned to laugh. There are times that I quite simply surprise myself…when I hear myself spontaneously laugh…it makes me joyful, because for me it is a sign of healing! For years, I could not laugh even at silly jokes. I could not see the humor in them.

It has been quite the journey for me, one that I will forever stay attentive to.

# Chapter 2

# The Woman I Love...Is Me!

How could this have happened? Why was I not strong enough to stop it? A million what ifs have colored my world for far too long?

On my journey to recovery, I have made many mistakes, HUGE mistakes. Missed many opportunities, sabotaged my own best interests. Stumbled and failed, got back up, dusted off my bruises, my aches and grew...grew to love myself.

If I cannot love me, how can anyone else love me? And truly, if I cannot love me, how can I wholeheartedly love another?

I AM The Woman I Love! Once I understood that I needed to love myself, that I could change not one thing from my past, things began to shift for me.

The beauty is that I discovered that I, in spite of all that transpired, did not lose that pure and beautiful little girl inside me. I really love her grit and determination, and the fact that despite it all, she kept peeking out from under the guise, the protective shield...and she smiles.

This is a quote from the works of <u>Louise Hay</u> that will set the tone of the story I am about to tell.

*"It doesn't matter how old you are, there is a little child within who needs love and acceptance. If you're a woman, no matter how self-reliant you are, you have a little girl who's very tender and needs help. If you're a man, no matter how macho you are, you still have a little boy inside who craves warmth and affection.*

*As children, when something went wrong, we tended to believe that there was something wrong with us. Children develop the idea that if they could only do it right, then parents and caregivers would love them, and they wouldn't punish them. In time, the child believes,* **There is something wrong with me. I'm not good enough.**

*As we grow older, we carry these false beliefs with us. We learn to reject ourselves. There is a parent inside each of us, as well as a child. And most of the time, the parent scolds the child—almost nonstop! If we listen to our inner dialogue, we can hear the scolding. We can hear the parent tell the child what it is doing wrong or how it is not good enough. We need to allow our parent to become more nurturing to our child.*

### Heal the Hurts of the Past

*I have found that working with the inner child is most valuable in helping to heal the hurts of the past. At this point in our lives—right now—we need to begin to make ourselves whole and accept every part of who we are. We need to communicate with our inner child and let it know that we accept the part that did all the stupid things, the part that was funny looking, the part that was scared, the part that was very foolish and silly—every single part of ourselves.*

### Love Heals

*Love is the greatest healing power I know. Love can heal even the deepest and most painful memories because love brings the light of understanding to the dark corners of our mind. No matter how painful our early childhood was, loving our inner child now will help us to heal it. In the privacy of our own minds we can make new choices and think new thoughts. Thoughts of forgiveness and love for our inner child will open pathways, and the Universe will support us in our efforts."*

http://www.healyourlife.com/love-your-inner-child

It has not always been this way for me. I have worked hard to stay in tune with my '*aha*' moments, as I work my way through my past. I remain forever grateful to both the intuitive souls that cared to write the words of encouragement that I've read over the years, some of which I share throughout this book, as well as the friends and angels that have crossed my path, and helped shed the light I needed to see.

> *"For all those who believed me, and for all those who didn't. It can't be easy hearing things you shouldn't."*
>
> Icarus X

This little girl kept reminding me that NOW is the time to let it out...it is time to play!

*"Loving me is the most important thing I could ever do for myself."*

As I share this story with you, I want to be clear that I am not writing it so that you will feel sorry for me. A "poor me" attitude does not cut it for me and is not part of the motive and drive to share this with the world.

I look at it this way: I have one of three choices I can make:

1. I can let it destroy me and leave me paralyzed.
2. I can let it change me to become or continue to feel less than and angry as well as destroy my dreams.
3. I can let it ignite my life and become a force for change.

I can honestly say there have been different times and stages in my life where I have chosen one or the other of the choices above, in fact, I have chosen all three! I suspect it is this way for many of us who have suffered the pain and suffering of abuse.

What I will say here is that for me, forgiveness and loving ME has been the answer. I acknowledge my own role in what I am about to share with you. However, know too that there are many blessings, gifts, and understandings that come our way, no matter how dark, if only we let it come to us.

Know that forgiving is not about forgetting what happened, or condoning the actions of another. It is about moving forward, healing and expanding your life in a way where you truly live!

I am **not** a trained therapist, I hold no degrees in psychology, and I am not equipped to counsel others who are struggling to break free. I am not qualified to offer anything but the sharing of my own experience. It has been in the telling of my story that I have been able to rid myself of the nagging depression, the anger, the debilitating self criticism and finally find inner peace and healing.

It certainly has not happened overnight. Know that time is a healer, and that it takes diligence to open your heart to healing.

I have put off writing this book for several years, even though I named this book, and reserved the website www.TheWomanILove.com several years ago.

This is a tough story for me to tell on so many levels. I have had to put aside the worries about what others will think of me if I tell my story. I have had quite a struggle with how it will impact my family.

I have tried many times to ignore the promptings.

I have chosen to tell this story because I know and understand that there are *many* who have experienced abuse. I hope this story will help to show that we can rise above our "story" no matter how many years you lived it and no matter how gruesome it was...IF you have the will to "make it so."

At the heart of this book is the deep desire to share and support others who have suffered abuse in the hopes that my story will shed light and give hope. If I can help even one person to have the courage to rise above a horrible situation, it is worth it to me.

Abuse comes in different forms and different degrees. I know mine definitely did.

As I weave this story of shame, humiliation, abuse, near breaking points, confusion and flat-out mind numbing fear, I have chosen to change the names of the important people in this narrative.

Each member of my family has our own journey and while we've each experienced abuses from the same source (our father), we are all uniquely different people, handling our pain and our recovery in very different ways.

I've always thought that as a family, those of us who survived would remain forever close. Sadly, that has been a near impossible feat, as we have all processed the abuse we experienced so differently from each other.

For my sisters; blame, finger pointing and denial has been the way to cope.

For my brother; immersion into religion and work consumes his life, as the pain is often too much to bear. My brother has lost two children...I am not sure many of us could feel whole and sane after enduring such grief.

My mother, now advancing in years, has grown stronger and healing is finally taking place for her. It's been difficult for me to accept her role in not protecting her children...in letting these horrible things happen. And yet, she too was a victim.

I will not go into graphic detail of what happened, as what I do share is going to be graphic enough. I also need to protect both the child...and the woman in me.

I remember as a child of eight, making the decision that I would not, could not, any longer remember everything that was happening to me. I refused to remember. It is a self-protection mechanism that kept me alive. Sometimes even today, I feel I suffer from that decision. I always have difficulty being able to convey a conversation I have heard, or even relaying information about an event that occurred. I feel it relates directly back to that decision I made so long ago.

As a child, and into adulthood, there were rules so abundant that it was mind splitting. Even more, there were stark contradictions, rampant hypocrisy, and a damaged soul that made choices for his life that adversely affected all who came near.

*And so my story begins.*

In order to heal, I must love myself. If I do not forgive both myself and those involved in this story, I lose.

Given the dark pains I've experienced, nothing is more generous and loving than the willingness to embrace grief in order to forgive.

I've decided that I no longer desire to keep this boxed away, and set aside. It has to die. It has to be grieved and released in a powerful decision to not simply survive, but thrive. I simply MUST love myself!

*"Don't let the darkness from your past block the light of joy in your present. What happened is done. Stop giving time to things which no longer exist, when there is so much joy to be found here and now."*

Karen Salmasohn

# Chapter 3

# A Bit of Background

As I sort through the weaving of this story, I will start with a bit of background as told to me in my childhood. This story was told consistently as I grew up...the truth or the merits of which I am unable to confirm. Anyone who could possibly confirm it has long since left our world.

As a child, my father himself was badly abused. Growing up on the streets as a child, he slept many a night in empty fields. To feed his siblings and himself, he often stole. He witnessed his father putting holes through walls in physically abusive acts towards his mother.

He was the second of four children, (one brother and two sisters) his parents divorced while he was very young. Alone, his mother resorted to prostitution. It was nothing for him and his siblings to witness, his mother cycle through several men in one evening. She married and divorced a number of men till she was in her later years.

At 10 he suffered a bad fall, breaking his neck and back, but his mom did not even notice until several days later. Even then, when she finally did take him to the doctor to get help, she simply dropped him off and went her way to more pressing commitments. He spent long months in casts, missing over a year of school.

He was in trouble with the law from a very young age. With next to no guidance, he took to a life of crime, mixing with older boys who were sowing their oats and likewise, had little or no upbringing.

His mother had no desire to be saddled with children. She eventually chose to lie about her son's age and name to enlist him at age 13 into the military. He was in Korea by 14, and out by 18.

I can still recall the stories of his experiences, the mistakes he made while on tour, and the older guys who looked out for him.

Meanwhile, at home she collected and spent his Class Q Allotment.

She introduced her daughters to prostitution while they were young as a way to bring in money to live on. While her daughters, my Aunts, later chose rich and productive lives to live, it was not without their own demons and pain-filled memories.

Upon getting out of the military, he made his way by going to Alaska to work the oil fields, and in that time met my mom's uncle who insisted he look up his niece should he ever return to California.

Two years later, he returned to California, and upon looking up mom's uncle, he was promptly invited to a family gathering where he met the 16 year old who was to become my mother.

Mom, a 4th generation born in Los Angeles, CA, has her own stories of abuse...and indeed abuse, like so many diseases passes on generationally. While she deeply cared for her own father, he was voiceless to the abuses met out by her mother.

*Musing: It is ironic that my mom's sister, my auntie, does not recall being brought up in an abusive household. My mother maintains that her sister was the favored child and resented her then and to this day does not have anything to do with her.*

And so begins this story of the union of a 17 year old girl and a 20 year old man. They had the same names, spelled differently, but pronounced the same way. As a child, I thought all parents had the same name!

This excessively handsome man was quick to anger, hostile, explosively volatile, demanding and controlling.

This young woman, graduated ahead of her class by six months, and married the day after graduation, had never learned to stand on her own. She took on a submissive role...never able to rise against the abuse meted out to her.

Her way of coping, even throughout my growing up years, was to be sick.

Not long after their marriage, the military knocked on his door insisting he needed to enlist. He adamantly refused. In the shortened version of this story, he had to go through court proceedings to prove he had indeed already served. The result was that he had to change his name back to his adoptive father's name to avoid reenlistment.

Within a very short time, they were the parents of two small children born 13 months apart. I was the second, born in 1956.

My brother and I are the 5th generation on my mom's side of the family to be born in California. Steve was born in Los Angeles, and I in a small mountain hospital in Northern California.

After my brother was born, my dad took a job at a saw mill in Northern California. However, not all was rosy for the newlyweds celebrating the birth of their first child, and preparing for the arrival of their second. In fact, during this time, my mom tried numerous times to terminate her pregnancy with me.

She was struggling with the abusiveness of her husband, raising my brother, and did not want to bring another child into the world.

She always told me that they were so poor that my bed was first a cardboard box, then a dresser drawer and said she was all alone, with no help from family.

*Musing: My aunt contradicts this story and says she and their dad were there to help for a solid month when I was born, and had brought a beautiful crib. I still shake my head at the differences of the story and do not understand the point of it.*

# Chapter 4

## My Early Years

So much of my very early years, well, most of my growing-up years, I simply cannot recall in any kind of detail. I am happy I can't!

There is one event that stands above all of my few earliest of memories and has been branded, no, seared into my memory as if it was yesterday.

I was not yet five years old. One of my many chores was to set the table for dinner. I remember circling the table after it was set, chanting "I will not cry," "I will not cry," *"I WILL NOT CRY"* over and over again.

Every evening when my father came in from work, I would cry. He hated it and it always ended up in beatings. This time was no different. He no sooner walked in the door and I started crying again. Again the beatings. His were not spankings, they were beatings.

After dinner was over, dishes washed and other chores were done, my brother and I were told we could go out and play. I decided this was my opportunity...I slipped out the back gate and ran...I was going to go far away from this place and from HIM!

Imagine a child of not quite five years, all by herself on the streets of Los Angeles! I had made it about 15 blocks away and stood petrified on a street corner without a clue of where to go or what to do.

An elderly couple out for their evening walk, happened upon me and inquired who I was and where were my parents and my home?

By this time I was shaking in my shoes...I was not supposed to talk to strangers...but I was SO scared. They were so kind. They insisted they needed to take me home.

I was beyond miserable and scared, knowing full well that I would be punished. They walked the 15 blocks back to where I lived with me...if you can imagine the look on my father's face when he opened the door!

As an adult, I realize that *that elderly couple were truly my angels*...what business did a small child have being off on her own at a tender age in a big city?

I look at my grandson who is nearing the age I was when I ran away, and I shudder to think of him walking the streets alone even in a "safe smaller community." I cannot imagine!

That night changed me. He decided me and him were going to stay up all night. He decided that if I was going to cry, then he would give me something to cry about. Each time I stopped crying, he would beat me again. And so it went till he left for work in the morning.

I no longer cried...outwardly, when he came home.

*Where was Mom? Why would she not come to my rescue? I feel certain that she tried, but she too was a victim.*

I was powerless to his violence and to his power. By the time the night was over I was broken. I was lost, and would stay lost for a long, long time to come.

I became the obedient, serving, hard-working, "ugly," "stupid," "never going to amount to anything," "forever a failure" daughter, with such a complex I could not breathe. This was his constant descriptions of me. I was a nervous mess, an always jumping out of my skin, aiming to please little girl.

Years later, my mother would recount the times she had to lock us kids in the bedroom, and tell her parents and friends we could not come out because we were sick. Truth was, we'd been beaten, and the bruises would have given clues.

*Musing: Looking back, I well remember the confusion. My father had a split personality. He could charm anyone who came near. He entertained. He could be outrageously fun. He was a smart entrepreneur. He was hard working.*

*But...he could change at the snap of the fingers. Typically that change, that transformation, came in a split second and with quite the repercussions. Seldom if ever, would that change take place in front of anyone other than our family. That would change later, but not for a good many years.*

# Chapter 5

# The Adoption

Not long after marrying my mother and starting a family, my dad decided to reconnect with his own father. His father had remarried some years prior, and had a very sick wife. While this man was my grandfather, I have no memories of him.

My grandfather's stepdaughter lived with them and had, from what was known at the time, two little girls who she badly neglected. She was only 18 and these little girls were ten months and almost three.

My parents tried to give her a new start. They took her and her two little girls in and made it possible for her to go back to school. Sadly, it didn't work.

She decided to give her little girls up for adoption and my parents, knowing they couldn't bear to let them go, made the decision to adopt them.

The oldest, at almost three years old had never had eaten a bite of solid food, and was in fact still nursing along with her younger sister. I can only imagine what a change this was for her in particular. She was used to the attachment and attention of her mama…having still been breast fed till this time.

Every meal with solid foods she was required to eat, ended up in vomit right at the dinner table, meal after meal after meal for several years.

When my parents took them to the doctor, the doctor demanded to know what country these children were from as they were so badly malnourished. It took years for the oldest, who I will call Karen, (not her real name), to be well and even at that, she has had many health issues to this day into adulthood.

Both girls were born in the Los Angeles General Hospital and at the time that Karen was born, there was a serious outbreak of staph infections. She suffers from residuals of this condition to this day.

As we later learned, not only were these little girls related by marriage, they were actually by blood. The sad truth of the matter was that my grandfather was the biological father of these little girls!

And the sadder truth is that their mother had already adopted out (to other family members, in hushed secrecy) two other children (that I am aware of)…my grandfather also the father!

In doing the math, she must have been no more than 12 or 13 when she began having children!

So my two adopted younger sisters' are really my aunts!

Their mother disappeared into the woodwork and years later, when Karen decided to look her up, she made it known she had no desire to reconnect.

Karen also attempted to locate and establish a relationship with the older siblings but was likewise rejected by the families who had adopted them.

Karen and Sharon entered our world, becoming my sisters, and now not only were there six mouths to feed, but four children under the age of six.

*Chapter 6*

# Religion

My father was a searcher...and that search led to many different religions. Lutheran, Baptist, Rosicrucian, Pentecostal, Catholic, Mormon. I know there were more.

Each one he dove into with zest and enthusiasm, often rising quickly to positions of deacon or youth leader, even elder, (due to that incredible charm I spoke of earlier.)

He obtained a huge truck and would seek out donations of food and clothing to take for the poor in Mexico. I recall those trips. I recall the poverty, the simple meals with fresh made tortillas, cacti and beans. The homes we stayed in, the wonderful ocean we played in, the children we played with even though we did not speak the same language and as well as the friendships that lasted for several years. Even at such a young age, I saw the stark contrast of life and learned about giving.

The sad thing was that for each religion he chose, he would leave in sadness, disappointment, and ranting criticism. Meanwhile each of us, including my Mother was to accept and reject as he did.

We were to reject not only the religion we had grown to know, but the wonderful people we had become friends with.

I vividly remember the huge sign with big spotlights that he put up in our yard at Christmas time: "Wise Men Still Seek Christ."

Some years we could celebrate Christmas, some years not. Sometimes we girls could wear pants, sometimes we could not.

The lists of rules would grow and change unpredictably.

I remember vividly, my brother Steve and I having to memorize entire chapters of the Old Testament each week. If we did not get it right, there was the certain beating to follow.

Then there was NO religion.

Included in that change, came the constant ranting that religious people were nothing but hypocrites and liars.

All wars were wars brought on "in the name of God" and therefore religion was a farce...and so it went.

## Chapter 7

# My Sickness

For two years in a row, I got terribly sick with pneumonia. I was already in school, so I think it was when I was six and seven years old. I missed a lot of school...those two years, but was able to keep up because of school homework being sent home.

I remember the second time particularly. He took me reluctantly to the doctor, because he did not know what was wrong with me. I was put in unusual positions so they could take x-rays and do their examinations.

I hated it because I had to take my dress off in front of the doctor. I did not know it was the only way they could get a good x-ray.

I was miserable on both counts...fear and being sick.

The doctor was alarmed at how seriously ill I was and immediately insisted I be admitted to the hospital. A fight literally broke out between the doctor and my father, as my father refused to have me admitted.

The doctor called on the law who threatened him with imprisonment if I was not admitted to the hospital. Somehow...with his charm, wit and convincing he won out and took me home.

He was into healthy alternatives now...and HE would heal me. Off to the health food supermarket for a juicer and as much horseradish root he could find!

That was the most gruesome concoction I have ever had to drink. It made me throw up. My eyes burned, my nose ran. They mixed it with lemon and honey and ordered me to drink every last drop, time after time. If you have ever ground up horseradish, even the grinding can take the top of your head off, so I know it was not an easy task for my parents. I know I got better, but whew was that awful stuff!

*Musings: As I write this, I am struck with the spiral of contradictions that was the fiber of my life. From giving unselfishly to those in need, to natural self-healing health measures, to beatings and abuses too miserable to detail. From sweet and kind, to rampant abuse. This is the definition of insanity and the life that was mine!*

*Chapter 8*

# The Move

Being a man of change and constant searching, he decided that California was not a good place to raise a family. He felt there was too much pollution, too much crime, even way back in the mid 1960's.

*My thoughts are that the extended family, grandparents, aunts and uncles were starting to suspect something was not right and my father knew it. Their decision was to move us far away from family...and indeed, us kids from that time on, were raised without the possibility of the benefits of family looking out for us.*

My folks purchased property sight unseen in Central Oregon and made plans for the move. Just prior to the move, dad made a misstep on the ladder and broke his back a second time. He was a house painter now, a stark change from the talented machinist he had been, but he had an innate need to be an entrepreneur.

Life as we knew it was about to change. My parents purchased an old single wide trailer. We moved from bustling and fast paced Los Angeles to an acre of land in rural Central Oregon, with the nearest neighbor a mile away in any direction.

My father could not accompany us on this move because of back surgery.

My mom, a city girl, ended up in a new location...in the forest, at the base of the Cascade Mountain range with four children under nine years old, no electricity, no running water, having never been on her own. As the coyotes howled in the early evening hours, she had to manage her own fears and make do.

Dad arrived two weeks later, unable to work, in pain, still recovering and likewise facing the magnitude of no work, in a new location and none of the conveniences that quite naturally, we were all accustomed to.

Aside from feeding and clothing the family, we had no electricity and no running water. It took months for the electricity to be brought in. We obtained a big tank for hauling water for drinking, cooking and bathing.

Eventually a well was drilled...and oh what excitement that was! It was 410 feet deep and the best icy cold water I have ever tasted was in ample supply.

No more heating our bath water on the wood stove. Water changed our lives for the good. Now we added livestock and gardens and a lawn. And best of all, no more outhouse!

For us kids, it was quite the adventure.

Me? I loved it! To this day that is the absolute favorite place I have ever lived. It meant very hard work for us kids, as my father still was not able to hold down much of a job and he was determined to start up his house painting business in a brand new location, a brand new world.

We had to depend on welfare to see us through on more than one occasion.

We canned just about anything we could get our hands on. We would travel across the mountains to Eugene and Portland to pick blackberries, strawberries and other kinds of produce. We never froze the produce...always canned.

We would go behind the combines and harvest the potatoes left behind in the fields. We would can what we could, and store what we could in the root cellar us kids had dug.

My father hunted and we raised pigs, sheep, goats and chicken to keep food on the table.

We worked for my father on his painting jobs, even the youngest. Her job was to pick up nails left on the ground at the new construction job sites. Those nails and the scrap wood that was picked up were items we used to build our home!

To go to school, we had to walk a mile to the bus stop, before the long bus ride to school. There were gravel roads, but I enjoyed the freedom of running through the forest and beating my siblings to the bus stop. I was a top notch tomboy. I still had to wear dresses...and oh my goodness, I ripped so many of them as I played on my way to and from school.

Those school years meant a good 12 hours away from home due to the distance of the walk, the bus rides and the schools.

The winters were cold with lots of snow. We had delightful times making snowmen and sledding, and ice skating.

It meant spending summers and fall going into the forest to cut firewood. Firewood that needed to be cut, split, and stacked with precision. The land needed to be cleared, and a suitable home needed to be built.

It was a slow and gradual process, one done in increments. I remember the day when the mobile home was removed to make way for the remaining half of the home to be built.

I chuckle.

I thought that home was HUGE! Years later, when I took my own daughters to see where I spent part of my growing up years, I hardly recognized the house...it was so small!

Clothing for us kids, were a couple of outfits for the summer, warm jackets, gloves, scarves and caps for the winter, and 2 pair of shoes, which included snow boots. These were to last an entire year...which meant many stern lectures on caring for what we did have.

Despite it being an awesome place to live, with the view of the incredible mountain range our windows, the gorgeous Deschutes River flowing through our town, the crystal clear lakes, the hunting and fishing, life was still very, very difficult.

My father was often stressed and angry. Mom's way of dealing with it was to be sick...ALL the time!

My father suffered a lot with his back, and often I would come from school and find them both in bed.

At eight, I became the family caretaker. I was in charge of cooking all the meals, the housekeeping and chore management, including ensuring my dad's breakfast and lunch were made before he headed off to work.

Many days, I would come home cold and hungry after a 12 hour school day, only to cook dinner for everyone, and to clean up.

School homework was not tolerated at home. He felt that we had spent all day at school; if we could not get it done at school, then too bad…this was family time. Many times I finished up school work on the long bus ride home.

It was also my responsibility to make sure everything was cleaned up, with all chores assigned to my siblings inside and out completed. The penalty for chores not done was very tough.

If there wasn't a refrigerator full of beer, he would be mad, which meant beatings.

Since there was not running water and no sewer, the drainage from the dish washing went from the sink to big buckets outside that needed to be emptied daily. Before the water well was dug, our bathroom was an outhouse, and during the winter we were allowed "thunder mugs" in the house.

At the time, it was not unusual for the winters to get down to 20 degrees below zero. (I believe the weather patterns have changed and they do not have the same extremes in weather there now as when we lived there so many years ago.)

Each of us was assigned our chores and it was my responsibility to make sure those chores were done…no excuses. In fact, if you had a reason those chores were not completed it was considered nothing more than an excuse. It was considered disrespectful, rebellious, irresponsible, and would not be tolerated.

So when certain chores were not done in the time frame expected…I was beaten because I had not made sure that the chore was completed.

Often, though, it was much worse for the one who was assigned the chore. Often, there were no questions asked...just swift and harsh action.

For example, Karen was to make sure the drain water barrels from the kitchen sink were emptied. On one occasion, she did not get to that task in the morning before school because it had a layer of ice on it and we left by six a.m. When we arrived home, we both got beatings, but she also got her head dunked in that horrible bucket.

If the "thunder mugs" were not emptied in the morning before school, then yes, we would both get the beating, but the perpetrator would not get to use the "mug" for weeks, even if it was 20 below zero... they had to go to the outhouse.

Something was happening to me. His idea of a beating, since we had moved to this remote location, was to go to the wood pile and pick a stick. "If it is not good enough, I will pick it for you," was his constant threat. The minute he ordered, "Go get a stick," my first stop was the outhouse (or later the indoor bathroom), but often could not even get to the door before I was drenched from wetting myself.

Those beatings were gruesome...and I had no control. "Yellow river by I pee freely" was the taunt that was chanted. I could not help it, and that issue stayed with me well into adulthood. Let a stressful situation arise...I would immediately in front of all...pee. I was mortified beyond belief.

~~~~

Years later, in my early twenties, I had errands to run in the city. Cell phones were not available then, so if we were going to be even 5 minutes late, we had to call. That meant finding a pay phone.

Knowing the chores I was sent to accomplish were taking longer than anticipated, I spent 10 minutes walking across the mall to find a phone. When I phoned to inform my father, that things were not going as planned, he went into such a rage over the phone, that I was not keeping my word, that I peed, absolutely drenched myself right there in that busy mall...and I had to walk back across the mall to accomplish what I had set out to do, in slushy shoes and obviously wet pants. Didn't bode well in the self esteem department!

I had surgery to rectify the problem years later, and thankfully, those horrible stress filled abusive days are now long behind me.

On one occasion, Karen did not complete a chore in the time frame expected…and we all, including my mother, witnessed my father take a broom handle and break every toe on Karen's feet, then beat the snot out of her. We all had to count the hits…till it reached 100 strikes.

Minutes later, my grandparents on my mom's side surprised us with a visit from California. It was the middle of the summer and I often wonder how no one noticed that Karen was wearing long pants, sleeves and could scarcely walk. It was also to be the last time I saw them until well into adulthood.

*Musings: In recently speaking to my aunt about this, she said, "yes, my parents never wanted to rock the boat, they always simply looked the other way."*

As I witnessed the abuse happening to my siblings, especially the more extreme cases, I became even more determined to please. I also became withdrawn, petrified, and more a mess than I care to admit.

How I wish I could say that I was brave and strong and rebellious. I simply became more submissive…but paid for it dearly with the bouts of depression that became a common occurrence.

*"She couldn't feel her wings, but she knew they were there. So she built a ladder to the sky, and when she touched the clouds, she would remember how to fly."*

Atticus

# Chapter 9

## Something Else

But then, something else was happening.

Nightly around the dinner table, the conversation revolved around health and hygiene.

We girls were NOT to wear underwear to bed and pajamas were strictly prohibited. Only nightgowns were allowed. "The body needs to air and rejuvenate...if you keep yourself closed up with clothing, you will have huge health issues." You will get yeast infections and end up being totally unattractive to anybody who would ever in the future think they wanted a life with you.

I was only nine! I also started my periods at nine. My body was already developing and I was miserably self conscious.

By now, I had developed quite the knack for blocking out painful events. "Why was this happening?" "This is incredibly weird!" "I hate this...how do I escape this?" were my constant thoughts...but all I could draw back on was that incredibly awful night and what happened when I tried to run away when I was nearly five.

All I knew was what happened was bad, but I could not remember WHAT happened aside from the beatings.

*Musings: I spent much of my early life in a state of constant never ending overpowering FEAR. Fear is a gruesome thing. Fear restricts the very fiber of life. It nearly destroyed my life.*

Sadly, fear, grief and hopelessness caused me to, on more than one occasion; consider taking my own life to end the pain, even as a youngster.

About this time... one evening, my father invited a bunch of the local guys (business owners) to the house. Of course my mom was sick and in bed. I had been in bed for about 1/2 hour when they arrived and I was exhausted. I had been up since our typical 4:30 a.m. "time to rise and shine" announcement from my mom.

But this night, my father came to my room. I had already fallen asleep. "Get up!" he demanded, "I have guests! You not know that it is your job to serve my guests!" I quickly got up and headed for my dresser to put on underwear. "No! You do not need underwear! Get out here *NOW* and take care of my guests." Here I was, wearing a thin nightgown, and I was supposed to serve "his guests???"

I know I walked like an abnormal person, trying to hide my developing body. I was mortified beyond belief.

Why did those men stay? More importantly, why did they come back? When I was done serving refreshments, I went back to bed completely humiliated and cried myself to sleep....

*Musings: Where was my MOM?*

I recently read the following from a book written by Carolyn Myss that has helped me to understand why my Mom was always so sick. Now at 80, she is healthier (and happier) than she was when she was young. I am so pleased to acknowledge that.

*"I have since become convinced that when we define ourselves by our wounds, we burden and lose our physical and spiritual energy and open ourselves to the risk of illness.*

*Spiritual depression presents itself in much the same way as clinical depression— but not quite. The marks of distinction are crucial, yet hard for the untrained to recognize. They make the difference between interpreting the source of depression as a problem that may require medication or as a process of transformation that is best served by reflection, discussion of the stages of the dark night, and understanding the nature of mystical prayer.*

*I have met many people who have been treated for depression and other conditions when they were, in fact, in the deep stages of a spiritual crisis. Without the proper support, that crisis becomes misdirected into a problem with relationships, a problem with one's childhood, or a chronic malaise.*

*Spiritual crises are now a very real part of our spectrum of health challenges and we need to acknowledge them with the same authority as we do clinical depression."*

Caroline Myss

The sad thing is...it was so difficult to connect the dots...I was already such a mess!

My father always told me..."You deserve this, you have asked for this. You should know better than to behave so provocatively!"

*My heart SCREAMED WHY? I HATE THIS!*

Fear led me down paths the little girl in me would NEVER have chosen. Fear and grief and hopelessness caused me to on more than one occasion consider taking my own life to end the pain.

At this time in history, at least where my siblings and I were concerned, Child Protective Services was nonexistent. <u>Read this staggering report:</u>

*"Child sexual abuse impacts more Americans annually than cancer, AIDS, gun violence, LGBT inequality, and the mortgage crisis combined...this abuse that occurs in the institution that predates all others: the family.*

*Incest was the first form of institutional abuse, and it remains by far the most widespread.*

*Here are some statistics that should be familiar to us all, but aren't, either because they're too mind-boggling to be absorbed easily, or because they're not publicized enough. One in three-to-four girls, and one in five-to-seven boys are* <u>*sexually abused*</u> *before they turn 18,* <u>*an overwhelming*</u> <u>*incidence*</u> *of which happens within the family. These statistics are well known among industry professionals, who are often quick to add, "and this is a notoriously* <u>*underreported*</u> *crime."*

Below is some additional statistics from a different source:

*"Every 107 seconds a sexual assault occurs with approximately 293,000 victims of sexual assault each year, this is a shocking statistic.* <u>The Rape, Abuse</u> <u>and Incest National Network (RAINN)</u> *has* <u>published statistics</u> *which show that 44% of victims are under the age of 18. Most importantly, research shows that the majority of sexual abuse perpetrators know the child. This may be surprising especially since in schools there is a lot of teaching on the dangers of strangers and what children should do if approached by a stranger. It is even more shocking that 68% of sexual assaults are not reported to police and 98% of rapists will never spend a day in jail or prison."*

I can say that my own detection monitors are very high, and when I suspect something, goose bumps hit in massive proportions.

I do believe that awareness is much more than it used to be. The two reasons, well, come to think about it, THREE reasons, the ONLY reasons I write this book are:

1. To free my own "demons" and heal once and for all.
2. To create awareness
3. MOST IMPORTANTLY, to provide hope and a roadmap of resources for recovery for those who are going through or have gone through their own nightmares of abuse and need help, acknowledgement and support on their own road to recovery.

Bear in mind that abuse can come in many different forms...sexual, mental, physical, emotional and spiritual...and NONE can be ignored.

In trying to piece this together for myself, I read something that helped me put this into better perspective.

*"Abusive relationships exist because they provide enough rations of warmth, laughter, and affection to clutch onto like a security blanket in the heap of degradation. Scraps of love are food for an abusive relationship."*

Maggie Young

The key, in fact the life saving process in this is to forgive first and foremost yourself...and more importantly, to LOVE YOURSELF. This is so very difficult to do, but to me, these are the *ONLY* answers.

*"Healing isn't just about pain. It's about learning to love yourself. As you move from feeling like a victim to being a proud survivor, you will have glimmers of hope, pride and satisfaction. Those are natural by-products of healing."* Ellen Bass, *The Courage to Heal: A Guide for Women Survivors of Child Sexual Abuse*

Therefore, this book: The Woman I Love.

If you are a man...it could read: The Man I Love.

Regardless, having gone through the abuses, I can attest that it is SO hard to come to love YOU!

For me...this did not happen for a VERY long time, but I think in retrospect...inside, I reached for the clouds and perhaps that is the ONLY reason I am alive today. That little girl inside was still alive!

*"There are many heartfelt reasons for pushing our childhood sexual abuse to the edge of our lives and one amazing reason to embrace a healing journey: It reunites us with our shining, colorful, joyful spirit."* Jeanne McElvaney

It is so easy to blame yourself for what happened. It is a typical response by those who've experienced abuse. It is definitely what I did, and that is LUDICROUS!

*"The legacy of childhood sexual abuse can be devastating and often makes itself felt years after the abuse itself has stopped. If you're wondering whether something that happened such a long time ago could be the cause of problems you're experiencing now, you could be right. If someone else has suggested this to you, it can be very hard to accept, but they too could be right.*

*Child sexual abuse is a profound violation. It affects every part of a developing young person's life. Even if you were able to separate it in your mind from other parts of who you were at the time, it was and probably still is affecting you deeply. The lies told or implied by the abuser damage a child's sense of reality and their whole view of the world. They especially damage the child's sense of self, confidence and self-esteem which can have far-reaching implications for the adult survivor, affecting future relationships, career choices, health and happiness."*

http://www.dabs.uk.com/information/childhood-sexual-abuse-incest

My father always said: "Women who are raped, 9 times out of 10 brought it upon themselves and are themselves to blame. They should have behaved with better morals!" ***Really?***

*"When we are ready to let go of our old controls, we admit that we were powerless over the incest or abuse. We have often thought, 'If only I could have stopped it,' but we could not have stopped it. We let go of the 'if only' now and sit still with our stark powerlessness...In our surrender to powerlessness, we touch ourselves with the gift of truth."*

Maureen Brady, Beyond Survival:
A Writing Journey for Healing Childhood Sexual Abuse

# Chapter 10

# Religion...Again!

As I mentioned earlier...my father was a searching soul. He was building his painting business, when he landed some really good jobs fed to him by a contractor. This man was a Jehovah's Witness and in no time, he and my father connected. Soon his family of four children and our family of four children, all similar in ages, met together for bible studies.

I was ten years old, my brother eleven. Jehovah's Witnesses were strict in all areas, but especially in the area of morality. I think, for a time, my father found the missing link to what had been missing in his life. He found mentoring from the elders and for a time he sought to "live the life."

For us as a family, this meant HUGE changes once again.

Picture this, middle of fifth grade. Suddenly, I could no longer salute the flag, celebrate Christmas, or any other holidays for that matter. It also meant that I had to give up extracurricular activities...no band, no sports, no cheer, no games...no friends.

For older youngsters just graduating from high school, it meant imprisonment due to being "Conscientious Objectors" to the Vietnam War.

*"A conscientious objector is an "individual who has claimed the right to refuse to perform military service"*[1] *on the grounds of freedom of thought, conscience,*

*disability, and/or religion.*[2] *In general, conscientious objector status is only considered in the context of military* <u>conscription</u> *and is not applicable to volunteer military forces.*"

They had to reject defending their country based on the Bible commandments that said "thou shall not kill."

I found the kids who were the elder's daughters and sons in just as much a state of confusion as I was! At least (I thought), they could be my friends! But they did not have the "straight arrow, we will follow this religion to the T" father.

Enter a pivotal age in all children's lives when they were discovering themselves...and the often made choices that would not separate themselves from friends and popularity.

It meant, during the age of miniskirts, I was going to school in skirts that hit below the knee...coupled with bobby socks and saddle oxfords. At a time when these things mattered...I had to stick out like a sore thumb!

Many of these "witness" girls would go to school and roll up the skirts, participate in activities that I knew to be condemned by our religion and then come to the meetings held five hours a week...with skirts the right length and be lauded as "so good".

I tried so hard to fit in, but even within our new found religion...I could never get there.

No matter how I tried I did not know HOW or Where I fit...but from what I was learning...I was not pure! I had already violated the rules of morality and I could tell no one.

My reprieve in all of this was not in fellow witness classmates...it was in the older, wiser witness "grand parents" that I gravitated to.

While I never spilled the beans on the real reason for my lack of fitting in and lack of confidence, I found a huge measure of consolation and support from these fine people. They were my temporary escape. They were the grandparents I so needed and filled such a spot in my life. I am so grateful for those wonderful people and those moments. *They were my angels...*

Meanwhile, due to his magnetic personality and charm, my father quickly rose in the ranks of this religion...and in short order was an elder.

At the time, in this religion, the end of the world was coming in 1975. It meant that *all* were expected to forego the pleasures of the world. For many of the witness youth of that time, it meant either quitting school or not continuing on with advanced education. It was considered "worldly."

It also meant foregoing medical attention, such as dental care, etc. because, after all, the end of the world was nigh."

It meant every weekend and every school break was spent going door to door in an effort to convert people from the error of their ways so that they could "live eternally on a paradise earth."

My brother took to it like a fish to water. He lived, ate, drank and breathed this life. He was often lauded as the "young Timothy" from Bible stories. He would preach to everyone he came in contact with... including fellow classmates and teachers.

Each night he would come home to dinner and gloriously share his vast accomplishments. (In retrospect, I think it was his guise and protection from the beatings and senseless beratement he too experienced. It was his security blanket.)

I have never known whether his claims were true, but he sure got a lot of mileage out of it!

In the witness religion, we were taught that there were only 144,000 who would go to heaven. This was from the time of Jesus onward. These 144,000 would go to heaven and rule as kings and priests over the earth...after the end of the world.

After "Armageddon," only those who at lived the purest of lives as witnesses would be spared the eternal destruction and would survive to help make this earth a paradise.

People who had died since the time of creation would be resurrected to life on earth and given 1,000 years to conform to the life of purity on an earth made into a paradise.

If they did not conform, they would be judged by those 144,000 kings and priests and condemned to eternal death if they chose not to conform.

At this point in time, there were very few of that number left on earth, and once a year at their "Memorial" those few would be the only ones who could partake of the bread and wine.

The rest of us would be "observers." Over the centuries there were those of that "calling" who did not stay true, so they had to be replaced. My brother decided he was of that chosen few.

No one can tell me that it was not his guise and protection. In my family, and in the eyes of many of the congregation, he might as well have been God himself. It certainly spelled a measure of relief from abuse for him...at least for a number of years.

Being a year behind him in school, I would trail behind. It was common for my sisters and I, especially me since my brother and I were so close in age, (13 months), to be interrogated every single night at dinner about how many I "preached" to while at school.

I often lied...because I HATED it, and in fact experienced beatings, scoldings and chastisement for not living the life.

It was not uncommon to walk the long hallways at school with the boys bowing saying: "Here comes Jehovah's girl." And "what would happen if Martians came to our world? Steve would preach to them! Bet his sister would too!"

Meanwhile the roller coaster of contradiction and confusion ruled supreme in my life.

# Chapter 11

# Work, Work, Work

Sharon (the youngest), was becoming a fearless force to be reckoned with. She was a rebel and a constant challenge to my parents.

As kids will be kids, we still, especially when dad was at work, wanted nothing more than to be kids. That included the usual pranks and scraps that happen with siblings.

Endlessly, Mom would warn us that she was going to "tell Dad." She was not permitted to handle the discipline.

Each of us wished she would have just handled the situation... because the discipline that he felt was warranted was swift and harsh.

Meanwhile, I *LOVED* where we lived. The beautiful snow covered mountains, the rivers, lakes and gorgeous forests. I loved the pond that was a mile away from home that I could escape to so I could blissfully ice skate my cares away. I loved the lava flows and walking the water flumes. I loved my pine needle and twig forts. I loved the camping trips...the times when it seemed my father relaxed and enjoyed himself and was actually fun to be around.

Of course there was often other "friends" around, but it was fun. Those times were my piece of heaven, my escape.

My father was of the belief that WORK was the way to keep his children in line…so the moments of play and relaxation were few and far between, but we seized any chance we got.

We would move a huge woodpile one day, only to move it again days later. We would hand dig root cellars, build barns and sheds, take care of the livestock, and work with him in the painting business. In that mountainous rural setting with pine trees galore, the trees were kept trimmed, and it was unusual to find even one pine needle on the ground.

He loved to entertain, and our home was often filled with guests. He made homemade beer, root beer and amazing wine…and it was the go to "fun" place for many of those families of same faith.

In this religion, at the time, "bad association would spoil useful habits" so friends outside of the faith were highly frowned on. The only exception was if they were prospective converts, and they were engaging in our bible study programs.

Even though I was the "designated servant," it was often a great reprieve from the abuse. The abuse was still there, as often, if I was not front and center to serve and care for the guests, (I yearned to play with the other kids, and would try to slip away for brief moments) but it never paid.

*"I used to extinguish by the weight of living, but some days, indeed in brief moments, I was able to reach into myself, dust off my courage and ask myself, "Where's my fire?""*

(adapted from a quote by D. Foy)

## Chapter 12

# The Doubts and the Pain

Because of expectations, as I entered junior high school, I had begun to lose my enthusiasm for school. After all, the end of the world was nearing. I was informed by my father, that I would be quitting school at age 16 to spend 100 hours a month going door to door to save as many as could be saved before the end of the world.

Plus I was also expected to work full time in the family business and take care of my family. It felt like a noose around my neck.

School had always been (at least the immersion into the education part of school) had been a part of my escape. I still did not know how to be brave enough to escape.

There were plenty of family conversations at the dinner table nightly that centered on obedience and submission. Women were not to preach in front of men, nor pray in front of men, and most certainly not correct a man, even if it was their baptized under-age son!

I clearly remember my mother being chastised by one of the elders when she quietly pronounced a word my father attempted to read during a bible study. Because of his childhood, he never really learned to read till we became witnesses, and even as he progressed in his reading skills, he often blundered.

If we were to be caught "teaching or preaching" in front of a "brother" (man), even an underage male, we were sternly reproved. If the occasion warranted it, we could get away with it if we wore a head covering while the male was present. I had to wear a head scarf if I was teaching a bible study to women, if my brother was present! Women were to be in subjection to man at all times.

Ha! If you know me now, that would be laughable. Even with the magnificent husband I now have, that would be laughable.

But then it was serious business...and the kind of superiority that validated my father and his just under the surface violent disposition.

As I grew into my mid teens, I found my father to be increasingly possessive. I never had boyfriends. Not that I was not interested or did not want one...they would start to come around and then they mysteriously stayed away. Far away.

I thought it was because there was something horrifically wrong with me. After all, I was impure! *I suspect my father ran them off.*

The increasing confusion of emotions that happen during those teen years combined with a man who was supposed to be my protector, my father...continued to haunt me.

How could one person transform from abusive, explosive accusing rants that often lead to beatings to a really sweet and charming gentleman at the snap of the fingers?

How come every time he had a chance he would seek out opportunities to be alone with me?

I would go to get something from the root cellar, he would show up.

I would go to the barn to tend my goats and sheep, he would show up.

I would be in the sewing room, he would show up.

Then he would pour on the charm. Then he would caress me and tell me how much he loved me. Then he would compliment me on how beautiful I was.

*Then SNAP!*

He would sense my non-compliance and my struggle and wham!

The beatings...the beatings that I most feared.

This happened so much over my early adolescence. The mind-numbing, spirit-crushing berating and being told I was ugly beyond belief. "I would NEVER make it in life." That, I "needed" him to take care of me.

I feared those painful beatings, less than I feared the sweet and kind side he could show. By this time, I was mentally and emotionally destroyed. When did the sexual abuse start? I know they happened at a very young age…but I cannot pinpoint when. I can only attribute this to my deliberate attempts to forget, which, became my only protection.

Did it happen before that little girl tried to run away? Is that why the inability to stop crying?

The day came, *I DO REMEMBER,* at around age 11, when I shamefully and vividly consciously stopped constantly resisting… shamefully even in my own mind! Resisting never worked anyway. I know it happened many times before now…but this I remember as if it was yesterday.

I was not worth anything. I so wanted my father to love me, to be worth something. I wanted to actually mean something to him. I wanted the beatings to stop. I wanted him to stop telling me how ugly and stupid I was. I wanted him to say he was proud of me.

I remember that day so vividly. The day that I crumbled, stopped resisting and without a fight willingly let him have his way. Maybe if I just stopped fighting, this pain would end.

On this occasion, he grabbed me by my hair and pushed my head down to his unzipped pants, his man parts showing. He told me then, as he had numerous times before, that I was too stupid to know how to take care of a man. That it was his responsibility to teach me how to please a man, otherwise, I was in for a far worse fate than I could imagine.

I know he knew I had given up. He told me how proud he was of me. There were to be many advances by him, and I became quite adept at creating ways to avoid being alone with him. But there were a massive amount of times I did not succeed at avoidance…and each time I lost myself a little more.

57

This sickens me beyond belief. This story is NOT an easy one to tell. I am laying bare my soul.

I sold my soul, by ceasing to fight, in hopes of ending the pain. And even as I write this, it would be so easy to STOP right now…to quit even trying to tell this story.

For years, even into adulthood, it would have been far easier to accept the perception I had since childhood… *"It is all my fault! I deserved this."* But as I began to seek answers in my adult life, I knew that that such an attitude or mindset could not fly. Because then no one wins!

The doubts? What good was religion? This was supposed to be the only one true religion, making others lives BETTER!

What's with the hypocrisy, the cruelty and abuse, by this "elder" and the actions by others in the name of religion?

Yes, I know that there are good people and bad in EVERY arena of life, and religion is no exception. It just took me a while to "get" that!

*Musing: It would be easy to put this future book away and be done with it. It would be and easy to slip into remorse, in to self-defeating self-sabotage. That is going not happen! I have worked way too hard to get where I am today…so depression and remorse is not an option. I do not care to go there.*

I fear depression. My utmost dream and goal at this time of my life is to escape the pain and chains of depression. I choose not go there. I have spent way too much of my life there and I love feeling joyful and happy! Truth be told, writing this book, telling my story is wonderful medicine to my soul.

Yes, now I do have so much to be happy about! I deliberately make decisions daily to nourish and feed my spirit. I chose happiness. I choose to step into my own power. I have a fabulous husband. Great kids…grandkids, a business, friends and extended family. My life now is tremendously better than it was in my youth.

It is true that at unexpected times, something triggers…and then…I am there. I find I must be ever watchful and attentive so that if I do find myself slipping I have set measures so I do not stay there.

Recently, I went to a conference in San Diego. I went a day early to walk the ocean, put my feet in the sand and just enjoy peace and quiet.

We had just lost a fourth member of our family to suicide. (We've lost two family members each to suicide between both my husband's family and mine.) Suicide as you will understand later in this story, triggers reactions in me, and I really needed this time away as a deliberate distraction to nip my own inevitable depression in the bud. It made such a difference for me and I was able to quickly rise above it.

At the conference, I connected with friends I'd met some years ago. Most of us have similar businesses and have stayed in touch, grown and learned together. The interactions were priceless!

The day after the conference my fabulous friend Sue and I hung out. We went to breakfast at a beautiful seaside cafe in La Jolla, then went to old town San Diego.

As we walked the streets of old town, with all of its vendor booths, we happened across an elderly woman sitting at a table full of books. A. B. Curtiss is an author and one of her books grabbed my attention. It is called "Brain Switch Out of Depression: Break the Cycle of Despair."

It is an awesome book, suggesting a targeted system of simple mind exercises developed from neuroscience research and brain mapping. It works! Between the wonderful interactions from my friends, the loving support of my husband and children, as well as the book I mentioned above, I have been steadily finding more peace in my heart. Since using the techniques, I have been happily staying on top of the cycle.

*I do believe in angels! Both Sue and this elderly woman!*

I have been taking breaks from writing this book because it brings up so much. Excruciating memories that have slipped into the background, memories that I deliberately determined to FORGET come back.

Many of those memories, I will NOT talk about in this book. It would serve no good and is not necessary. What I have said and what I have yet to share before this book is complete is quite enough for you to get the picture.

I am determined to *LOVE MYSELF* and treat myself with tenderness and care. The child as well as the grown woman inside of me, needs to be cared for, loved and respected and it is my responsibility to do that.

My husband is right beside me, reading each little segment I write, ever watchful and concerned that I can handle this. He will be writing a chapter or so in this book, to share our journey in these nine years since we met. I have been blessed with an amazing man! *I always tell him he is my angel.*

This book is being written with the intention of healing. It is also being written to give hope.

Overcoming abuse does not just happen. It takes positive steps each and every day.

I am certain I do not own a corner on the market of the abuse that can happen, is happening or will continue to happen to many others, young or old, male or female even in this very moment. I am also fully aware that many have had it far worse, and in fact lost their lives due to abuse, or know someone who has.

My desire is to help create awareness of what a powerful blow **any** kind of abuse can be…and along with all the others who are speaking up, writing, and dealing with their own skeletons in the closet…**blow the lid off of it!**

The most profound thing that I have learned from my past is purely conveyed in this quote from Caroline Myss:

*"The inability to forgive is as painful as the wound itself."*

I know within every fiber of myself that I do not care to have just survived. I intend *to thrive* and more importantly, *be the change I want to see in this world.*

I am learning to let go, let live (and let die)…and above all FORGIVE. That forgiveness includes forgiving myself.

I have learned that I can *CHOOSE* to think in ways that will support my happiness and success…and I can accomplish that by loving myself so I can help to change the vibrational frequencies of abuse.

*"In order to benefit fully from the healing power of telling your story, you must resist from holding anything back. It is time to strip off the mask, forget what everyone else will think or say and tell it like it is without apology."*

# Chapter 13

# So Many Contradictions

*I*t feels like the family I grew up in lived two completely contradictory lives at the same time. Even as I write this book, I find it strikingly to be so.

My father had a generous and giving side that matched his magnetic, happy winsome handsome side, and as I reflect, I believe that there was where the confusion was for us kids and even my mom.

When he was happy, he could convince you that all was right in the world, that we were a completely normal family, shining examples in our congregation and a blessing to this world.

*I have this perception that all babies brought into this world start out good and pure. When do they make a choice to go the other way? It is a choice. We all get that choice. When did this happen for my father? When does it happen for anyone who commits acts of violence and hatred? I cannot believe they were born that way.*

The problem was...the unpredictable trigger switches for him.

The unpredictable things that would set him off into the mean, controlling, abusive, hateful ranting second side of him are difficult to describe, let alone understand. And generally, he was successful in making any one or all of us believe it was *OUR* fault, and we got what we deserved.

The amazing thing to me is that he often, at least in those years, did not display this to those outside his family. It was a daily dinner conversation that, what goes on within our family, stays within the walls of our family or there would be dire consequences. In later years, this meant death threats. I believed him!

In fact, no letters to friends or relatives could be written and sent without his first inspecting and revising to suit his taste.

All conversations with friends, "brothers and sisters" in the religion, including the ministerial servants and elders was to be kept from him.

We had to relay word for word what was said, who said what and why it was said. How many times our interrogations around the dinner table would last past midnight, even when we kids had to be up in at 4:30 a.m. so we could have our chores done before we headed off for school.

Those interrogations were mind splitting...and based on my own deliberate decision to forget things when I was eight...remembering word for word was a gruesome process.

By the time he finished interrogating, I could never be sure exactly what was said, I was now so confused. I could not remember especially when he took and twisted every word said into something that was not said.

To this day, I still have trouble remembering the exact words that were said in conversations I have today. I can repeat the "gist," but never the exact words.

*Chapter 14*

# Moving to "Where the Need was Greater"

The witness religion was focused on growth and encouraged upstanding members to "move where the need was greater" to help grow their ranks.

Our family was no exception. Our parents uprooted us from gorgeous central Oregon to beautiful Tennessee. We were being sent there to help integrate black and white in to one place of worship.

Here you have a West Coast family who had no experiences with racial prejudice, and we were placed in a rural Southern environment in the early 1970's, some 70 miles East of Memphis bordering Mississippi. This was the "Bible Belt." They wanted integration like we would want a hole in our head!

If you ever lived in the South, especially years ago, you will understand what I mean. There had been no training. No preparation for what we were getting ourselves into.

By this time I was 16 years old. I had already quit school, because "the end of the world" was near. To find a place to live, my parents had to be deceitful. They could not disclose their religion if they hoped to find a home to purchase.

My very first experience going door to door in this rural southern community was knocking on the door of a beautiful home. The man opened the door and I introduced my younger sister and myself, explaining that we were Jehovah's Witnesses.

The usual presentation was about how they too could gain "life eternal on a paradise earth." No dice with this guy! This man went into a rage!

He asked me point blank "would you marry a black man?" I had never considered even pondering the notion…and stood there dumbfounded. He asked me, "Have you ever seen a horse mate with a cow? Well, have you?" to which I stupidly replied, "No, I haven't, but I have seen brown cows mate with white cows."

He kept yelling at me, repeating the question and demanding I answer. Finally, I said, "well, I suppose if I loved the man, I would." (Thou shall not lie) *WRONG!!!*

To this day, I am not sure how we made it off his porch alive, and over the course of the next eight years, experienced many occasions of guns being pulled on us over the same issues. Needless to say, I got much smarter in my answers!

Tennessee is an amazing contradiction of a place to live, with lush green, and a noisy beauty only found in the South. But they, at least in that time, were still fighting the civil war!

The beautiful mansions, often depicted in movies like "Gone with the Wind" were breath taking. But should one approach the front door accompanied by a person of color? Best not…if you even dared approach, it was best to go to the back door, but that was frowned upon by the witnesses.

One situation taught me so much about the repercussions and criticalness of racial prejudice. There was a young woman, who was likewise sent from Oregon, to "serve where the need is great." She came to the same congregation we were assigned to. Only she was barely 18 and by herself. She stayed with a witness family recently transplanted from California, also called to "serve."

As was customary, our assigned car groups of "pioneers" sent to spread the message was a mixed group of black and white. Often there would be a group of six of us, our "territory" being the rural back woods of Tennessee and across the State line into Mississippi.

Generally our little group would include a dashingly handsome young black man with a fun and cheerful personality...and Sarah. Sarah and Johnny fell in love with each other, and decided to marry.

The horrible things those two young people had to endure. Nobody would rent to them. They had stayed with Johnny's family for a short time, but the combination of a rat infested home and the pressures heaped on the family was too much. Johnny and Sarah ended up living in their car.

Pregnant, harassed and scared out of their minds, they finally had to move far away if they wanted to have even a sliver of chance of staying alive. They had received numerous death threats. This was the painful reality of life in the South.

Now I understood why the answer I gave the man whose door I knocked on the first week I lived in Tennessee was so very unwise.

I've watched many movies depicting life in the South, like "The Help" and their depictions were very vividly true.

I met many wonderful people.

There was one elderly black woman who had been a slave as a very young child. She had escaped to Chicago as a young woman, was educated and very talented. She returned as an older woman to take care of her mother...and so many years later still daily transferred her shoes left to right, so they would not wear out so quickly. She still remembered the beatings and abuse and would tell of her days of slavery.

This was in the 70's. Cotton and soybeans were main staples, and it was not uncommon to see the cotton being hand harvested by people of color.

Our congregations grew...grew from transplanted witness families and many people of color joining our ranks. Getting whites to join was another thing. It happened, but very slowly. Along with this came an entirely new set of problems, including deep set prejudices on both sides of the racial spectrum.

One particular Saturday morning, I was the assigned driver. I was assigned two black ladies, two young black girls and my younger sister. We were assigned to one of the toughest, all-black ghetto neighborhoods in the area. So with trepidation in my sister and my hearts, we enter the neighborhood. As we were instructed, we were to go to the doors, in mixed sets.

The black "sisters" were comfortable. They were not fearful. But at each door, men were making passes at us white girls. They were jeering, taunting and threatening.

I made the decision that we were not safe, and told everyone to get back into the car.

One of the black sisters then accused me of being prejudiced. I insisted that I was not, that if this kind of conduct happened in an all white neighborhood, I would have made the same decision. I told them that since I was the assigned "car captain," I was responsible for all of our safety.

I was so hurt when I got called before the elders with charges of prejudice! They offered to remove me of my "pioneering" status and be put on reproof before the entire congregation should such a thing ever occur again.

In our "door-to-door" work we often came across secret cemeteries where babies from white men impregnating young black women were buried. It was very common.

One lady with her family of six was 12 when she got pregnant with her oldest child, a daughter. Her daughter in turn had her first child at 12. Can you even imagine being a grandmother at 24? In the South this was so prevalent.

Where we lived in Tennessee was beautiful, I always referred to it as a noisy beauty. The spring would regal us with the smell of wild musketdines that had the aroma of grapes. The dogwood, lilac and tulip trees and a vast array of colorful wild flowers created a symphony of color. Because of the abundance of green and water, the birds provided a constant symphony.

We had amazing gardens that never had to be watered, due to the amount of rainfall we got there.

We grew and canned all our own food. We harvested our own corn, tomatoes, peppers, potatoes, beans, onions, garlic and more. We also grew our own peanuts. Yum...the peanut brittle we made from those peanuts. Fresh harvested peanuts are nothing like the peanuts we purchase in stores today.

We were surrounded by cotton and soybean crops. We had livestock. My job was to milk the cows...then take care of the milk. I learned how to make cheese, cottage cheese, buttermilk. I learned how to cook all kinds of amazing foods. I spent a lot of time sewing for myself and my family.

The summers were hot and humid, the winters with lots of rain and occasional ice storms, and the spring was always heavy storms and frightening tornadoes.

# Chapter 15

# Stresses of a "Grown-Up" Family

*"We do not choose to be born. We do not choose our parent, or the country of our birth. We do not, (most of us), choose to die; nor do we choose the conditions of our death. But within the realm of choicelessness, we do choose how we live."*

Joseph Epstein

While experiencing the changes of an incredibly different world, there was the same set of problems and challenges, only with a great deal of other stresses.

My father was the main "elder" and pretty much out of his element dealing with a huge set of new circumstances that came with moving to the South.

The stress at home was compounded with the responsibilities he had with the religion, and making a living in a new location.

House painting continued as the family business. We would be up at 4:30 a.m., chores done, and out the door to Memphis to paint track homes being built.

It was a great contract that provided well for us. Even though I had worked in the family business when we lived in Oregon…now I was earning my own pay check!

Just before we moved here, a young woman going through difficult times with her family, who were not witnesses, was invited to join us. Her and my brother had a thing for each other.

This opened a whole new can of worms.

Now, on top of everything, nightly discussions about being chaste, keeping our virginity and behaving in a proper manner with the opposite sex were consistently hammered into our heads.

Really? How was I to take this? I found myself secretly seething, angry, moody. What was this? But I never dared to spill the beans.

In this religion, sex outside was punishable. At no time was a couple to be alone together. They must always be chaperoned. My father took this to extremes. It just about drove me nuts. (How did this compute? This was double standards!)

Each time my brother and Sally tried to sneak of for even just a few minutes, I was instructed to "on the double" follow them.

Now, answer me this: Just how does a couple determine they are right for each other, that they are truly compatible if they never have alone time?

Where was the trust? Where was the responsibility? Where was spontaneity?

A much larger question was why were there two sets of rules? Why could my father arbitrarily make these rules, yet break even more important rules, and violate the most sacred?

By now, he resorted to tactics that kept me perplexed and nervous, always looking over my shoulder. He threatened me that if I ever told, he would kill me. I believed him.

*Musing: My father was of German-Jewish descent. I could only relate to this in the light of what happened for the Jews under Hitler's rule. How many otherwise good people did the unspeakable under Hitler's spell to save themselves and their families?*

It is insane. In my mind, my father was much like Hitler. He could rule with an iron fist and I had observed many otherwise good and sensible people, both men and women, crumble and succumb to his demands, no matter what those demands were or who they themselves were. He had an odd power that many succumbed to. I witnessed adult men succumb to his power!

The odd thing is that watching even full grown adults bow and scrape to him, gave me inklings of hope that maybe I could somehow, someday rise above this. I was beginning to learn that our family was NOT normal and that not all fathers treated their daughters in such a way as he had treated me.

He always said I was "too stupid to make it out in the real world." "I was so ugly, no man would have me." By now, I was convinced. No really good man in the Witness religion would have me. They wanted and expected a virgin…and my deep dark secret was that I was NOT a virgin.

In those yearning quiet moments, I sought to figure it all out. I knew that I could not marry outside of the religion, as that was forbidden. But, I also did not want to go down the same path as my brother and his wife, of constant chaperoning during courtship.

While there were young men in the witness religion, I had yet to meet one I felt it was worth going through that agony.

There were a lot of female witnesses, and few young male witnesses. I felt that the few young men that were available, were conceited with big heads, because the girls were constantly hounding them. I feared the same treatment from them as I had experienced from my father.

My heart was drifting away, but it would be years yet before I mustered the courage to listen to my heart.

I was always sad. I wanted to be married, to have children, to belong and to be loved. But those haunting words constantly echoed inside of me.

Meanwhile I buried myself in work…I had not yet learned that life is not about waiting for the storm to pass. It is about learning how to dance in the rain.

*"Many of us learned that keeping busy kept us at a distance from our feelings. Some of us took the ways we busied ourselves—becoming overachievers and workaholics—as self esteem. But whenever our inner feelings did not match our outer surface, we were doing a disservice…if stopping to rest meant being barraged with this discrepancy, no wonder we were reluctant to cease our obsessive activity."*

–Maureen Brady, Beyond Survival:

A Writing Journal for Healing Childhood Sexual Abuse.

In this case, until I had the courage to make drastic changes, the storm would never pass!

My father demanded that my brother and his now fiancé get married right away. He did not want the stress of making sure they stayed pure. So in short order we had a wedding planned. I made all the dresses and because they had no money, I decided to make the flower bouquets from wild flowers.

I have to laugh simply recalling that wedding. The morning of the wedding, I picked all the flowers and arranged them. Since it was an April wedding, there was an abundance of daffodils, iris, and other kinds of flowers.

I took the flowers to the "Kingdom Hall" and put them in one of the small rooms, so I could return home and dress for the wedding. The day started to turn chilly, so the first ones arriving at the hall for the wedding turned up the heat. For some reason, the heat was turned up high and when we returned for the ceremony, the flowers were wilted! While it was kind of funny, my poor sister-in-law was beyond disappointed.

My brother and his new wife, who were pretty much my best friends, moved to another city. We had spent so much time together. Now they were gone, starting a life of their own, and not there to be my buffer.

Because there had been five teenagers in the house, financially, there was no way that 3 could be driving at the same time. With my brother and his wife out of the house, I finally got to learn to drive, and get my own set of wheels.

My first car was a brand new bright red Mazda, with a stick shift, no air conditioning and black vinyl upholstery. I purchased it on my own through a loan from the local bank and paid it off a full year early.

I loved having my own set of wheels, and found opportunities to spread my wings as much as was allowed and was possible.

I often wondered about my brother and sister in law. While they ended up moving back to our town, in fact at a certain point they began living on the same property in a mobile home they had purchased, they certainly seemed an unsuited pair.

Would they have married each other if they had had a chance to be alone and truly get to know each other?

In that religion the only grounds for divorce was if one mate committed adultery. So they stayed married, had 4 children and many years of turbulence and unhappiness.

*Chapter 16*

# *Serious Troubles*

The prejudice in Tennessee, the "Bible belt," was still a major issue and we had for several years, been plagued with pranks, especially at Halloween time.

This one year, it got really serious. We had been away for a witness convention, and did not return till it was already dark on this particular Halloween evening. Witnesses do not celebrate any of the holidays… Halloween included.

When we arrived, there was wet paint plastered all over the house and yard, mixed with confetti and firecrackers and dead animals. Plants had been crushed, sidewalks and porch a gooey mess.

It was scary! I remember cleaning up the walkway, and with a full bucket of trash headed to the backyard to dump the bucket into the burn barrel. As soon as I did, the still smoldering barrel started popping and crackling from all the fire crackers I'd swept up.

I hit the ground in a panic, at first not realizing the cause of all the pops. My heart must have beaten outside my chest; it took me a while to recover.

Later that night, after we'd cleaned up as much as we could, and gone inside preparing for bed, there was a sea of men's voices and raucous outside our home. My bedroom was up stairs, I turned out the lights so I could peek out.

What I witnessed will haunt me to this day. It was the Ku Klux Klan placing a huge wooden cross in the front yard. On the cross was an effigy of a fully dressed man with a huge nail stuck in the heart.

They yelled: "You will be next! Take heed. We want you out of our town!"

After that, for us girls to be out, we had to have CB's in our cars and we had 24 hour FBI surveillance. It was not a fun position to be in, and truly nerve wracking.

Finally, after tons of discussions and pleading, my parents decided that it was no longer safe to live there. They put the house and property up for sale. The locals threw a boycott, so nobody would even look at the place.

The tensions and fear for our lives was very real, so we finally let it go to auction. We pretty much lost everything ending up with barely enough to start over again.

Before we left, we had all been away at one of our Bible Study meetings at the Kingdom Hall. My parents for some reason had gone to that meeting in their own car, likely because they needed to give somebody a ride to the meeting. I had driven my car with my sisters. After the meeting was over, my sisters and I decided to leave earlier than my folks, because we had been working all day and my father still had elder responsibilities to handle. We took off. There were miles of back roads to travel to get home.

Suddenly there is a car behind us, bright lights on and traveling fast. This car was right on our bumper. I attempted to pull over so it could pass, but the driver pulled over too.

We were beyond petrified. The driver kept the bright lights on and honking...I was having trouble seeing because of the lights. I tried speeding up, a dangerous thing to do on winding narrow rural, country back roads. I tried slowing down. I tried ditching him with a quick maneuver onto a side road at the last minute.

It was nearing midnight, no street lights. I had no idea what to do. As we neared home, I told my sisters to prepare to run. I would pull all the way up in the drive way to the back of the house. The back door was very close to the driveway; they should make a run for it, get inside and call the police.

That plan did not work. The car that had been following us pulled in, likewise all the way to the back, and stopped not even 1/2 inch from hitting my car...horn blaring. I honestly thought we were as good as dead.

Then we hear hysterical laughing from my father. I was so mad and frightened I screamed at him...the first time I had ever raised my voice towards him.

He proceeded to say what idiots we were (especially me, the eldest), that I could have been responsible for my own and my sisters' rape and death, that it could just of easily be the Ku Klux Klan.

He said we should have driven the additional twenty miles to the police station and honked the horn till help came. We'd tried the CB, but could not get help.

He may have been right that the smart thing to do was to keep driving to the police station, but hell!

By the time he stopped ranting, raving and laughing at us it was 2 in the morning and we were expected to be up and ready for work at 4:30.

*Chapter 17*

# Sharon

By now my Karen was old enough to quit school at 16 and also pioneer. I was expected to teach her the routine. I really did not like going door to door. I also had to teach both Karen and Sharon how to drive.

Pioneering (preaching door to door 100 hours a month) was not in my heart…but it was expected. So I continued on, with a heart that was not at peace.

I mentioned earlier that my youngest sister, Sharon had a mind of her own and was quite the rebel. When the three of us girls were together she was snarly and obstinate, and given to fits of rage. She was difficult to handle. There were times when I wanted to order her to get out of my car and walk home because of the stunts she would pull.

Sharon was my baby sister. Petite and cute, I had always loved doting over her and making her beautiful dresses.

But she was made of something different than I was made of. Early after our move to Tennessee, friends came from Oregon.

They were our neighbors, my parent's first converts into the witness religion. They had 7 kids, the second from last was named Omega (meaning "last"), then the youngest born two years later, with the initials, P.S.

The dad of this family had always been my ally. At great risk to himself, he would often step in and run interference on my behalf when he observed my father being insanely tough on me.

I will never know if he understood the full scope of what was truly happening to me and my siblings, but for me he was my idol. So many times, he could sense my despair and get me laughing by his crazy antics. I will always treasure this man, even though over the ensuing years we have seldom been in touch.

Anyway, our parents had been the best of friends, and it was not unusual to have them (all 9 of them) make the long drive to Tennessee, or our family, in return make the long drive back to Oregon…without first letting each other know. We or they would be showing up on each others' doorstep.

It brought many a laugh for all of us, and I am certain a fair amount of stress for the parents.

At any rate, on one last of these visits, the parents needed to "speak" with my parents. Evidently, Sharon had engaged in "improper conduct" with their oldest son. They were about the same age…maybe 12 or 13 years of age when it had happened, and their son had disclosed the information to them.

This was just the beginning. Sharon was always in trouble. She stole, she lied, and she did all kinds of things at school that equated to improper conduct for a witness.

In the witness religion, improper conduct was exposed…in front of the congregation. First there would be a "talk" given by the elders (generally my father) to the entire congregation, that a situation had arisen and how wrong it was, and what it could lead to. No names were mentioned, just warnings.

Next there would be 'public reproof' which meant that the act of misconduct was exposed to the entire congregation, and the perpetrators were named. The entire congregation could still 'associate' with the perpetrators, but only in a "religious" environment. They could not be associated with on a social/friendship basis.

Then, if the bad conduct persisted, or as the term was, they were not "repentant," there was disfellowshipping.

In this case, not only was the offense described, the names of those involved were announced, and it was strictly enforced that we could in no way associate with these individuals.

We could not speak to them, we could have any association whatsoever, lest we suffer the same fate. After all, bad associations, spoil useful habits. The idea was supposedly to shame them into repentance.

Well, Sharon was not of age, (she was not even 16), so my father decided to not take her issues to the congregation. He simply demanded that none of us, her siblings could speak to her. She was to be ignored within the family at all costs. She still lived in our home, but was treated with scorn and totally unequivocally ignored.

Instead of making an impact on her, she dug in her heels and got in more trouble every day. I think she invented ways to get into trouble!

My father forbade us to even give her a smile, a whisper of encouragement. He was beyond hateful to her and finally decided she needed to be removed from our home.

He called another witness family who lived several states away. They were a family of 3 boys, one of whom was her age. He asked that they accept her into their home in hope that this would be a wakeup call. They accepted.

Well, it backfired, because within 3 months we got word that she was pregnant out of wedlock. My father was beyond enraged. She dug her heels, even more stubborn.

As her siblings, we were threatened with insane repercussions if we ever spoke to her, even the threat that all of us would be killed.

Things with my father had progressed to the point that we were each fully aware that his threats could easily be executed.

She married, went on to have four more kids and I have personally never seen her again. I know she has been married and divorced several times.

I spoke to her several times over the years, the last time we spoke she said that she desired no contact with me, because I did not protect her. There was less than 4 years difference in our age, but she said she held me responsible, because I had been the only mom she ever knew.

While I've tried to be big enough to understand her viewpoint, I was deeply hurt. I hadn't even been strong enough to protect myself, and that was a massively strong burden to bear.

It was in the latter years of living in Tennessee, that my brother and father started a new business together. This was a saw blade sharpening business, and my father's early in life machinist skills help them develop the business into something quite profitable.

It would stay in our family for years to come. My father was suffering with his back injuries, and lifting the heavy paint buckets and ladders was becoming impossible. The humidity of the South also had a detrimental effect on him.

In the meantime, I started my own business. At first, I hung wallpaper in homes, did small painting jobs, and cleaned homes and apartments after people moved out.

Then my sister and I started a very profitable lawn mowing business. We had quite the routine.

After that I moved into something I totally enjoyed…it was called Busy Bee Business, and I did specialized floral arrangements for high end weddings and special events. I found my calling in the beautiful creations I made!

*Chapter 18*

# Reflections

*Musings: Inside us, there is something greater than what we know. We just need to release it.*

*"Faith is like wi-fi...it is invisible, but has the power to connect you to what you need."*

My adult life has been one of discovery and searching for what that something greater is. *How was I to live in each moment without regrets? How was I to recover and be whole?*

Even writing this book is my journey to wellness in all areas of my life. I have a story to tell, to release, as part of my healing process. For anyone who has gone through any measure of abuse, the healing is an ongoing process, and one that cannot be ignored.

I constantly have to remind myself that I must live in the NOW.

I can do *absolutely nothing* to change the past....*NOTHING.*

I choose to live well now. I choose to be the change I want to see in our world, and pave the way for an amazing tomorrow.

All we have is today. Situations arise in life that spark triggers of emotion and regret, watch for them, acknowledge them and rise above it.

*The same boiling water that softens potatoes hardens eggs.* It is all about what we are made of, not our circumstances.

As I try to make sense of all of this, I recognize the fact that when you begin life in this kind of world as an infant, and you grow up in that environment, and are kept isolated from what life could truly be like…you come to think of your experiences as normal…isn't this what happens in EVERY family?

It is comparable to the analogy of the frog placed in boiling water. Because of the drastic temperature difference, he jumps out immediately. But put the frog in cool water, and ever so slowly turn up the heat, he adapts…and soon he is cooked!

We were isolated from relatives. We were not allowed sleepovers with friends. Seldom did we get just kid time. When we did get time to play, those times were few and far between and seldom with other kids.

While we did go to school, especially from the time we became Jehovah's Witnesses, we were constantly reminded that; "bad association spoils useful habits." We were constantly reminded that our role at school was to be 'spreading the message of "truth."

What did we have to compare with, except from that voice from deep within that kept screaming out? Innately we know there is something wrong…but what can a child do about it? Inherently, the deep ache in my heart, kept telling me there was something darkly wrong.

Although it was not the "rules" of the religion, we did not get to listen to music, watch T.V., nor go to movies!

I have beat myself up regularly about WHY I stayed. Why I didn't try to run away again. Why I did not take some kind of action. Because was paralyzed by fear.

*"I must say a word about fear. It is life's only true opponent.* **Only fear can defeat life.** *It is a clever, treacherous adversary, how well I know. It has no decency, respects no law or convention, shows no mercy. It goes for your weakest spot, which it finds with unnerving ease. It begins in your mind, always ... so you must fight hard to express it. You must fight hard to shine the light of words upon it. Because if you don't, if your fear becomes a wordless darkness that you avoid, perhaps even manage to forget, you open yourself to further attacks of fear because you never truly fought the opponent who defeated you."*

– Yann Martel, Life of Pi

# Chapter 19

## Another Move

This next segment of my story is the truly the most difficult to talk about. It is starkly humiliating. It is why I've kept stalling in writing this book.

Yet, to free myself of the "demons" and shed light on what I suspect affects MANY women, it is imperative that I release this to the universe.

I've anguished over this for so long, and it has truly colored my world. While I am happy with the ending of this story, it is what happened to get to that point that has haunted me in unbelievable ways.

We moved to Arizona, as the place of choice for my father due to his always being in pain from his back and neck injuries. The humid conditions of Tennessee had been a constant nuisance for his health. My brother, his very pregnant wife and their first child moved with us. After the auction in Tennessee, we were hugely strapped financially.

We purchased a very old house in a small Arizona town that had a machinist shop and land right in the heart of the town. This was perfect for the business my father and brother had begun in Tennessee.

I did NOT like Arizona! It was barren and dry and HOT!!! We moved there at the end of May, with no time to adjust to the massive heat. Dust storms and monsoon summers were not my idea of beauty.

Oddly, over the years, most all of my family left Arizona…and I remained!

We settled into the witness life in the small congregation that was there…only this time, I seemed to fit in with the young people who were members, a bunch of us all around the same age. Myself, and most of the others were also full time "pioneers" going out preaching door to door at least 100 hours a month.

We had lots of fun together. We traveled together, had parties, went skating, cooked together and started experiencing things I never got to do before. Those friendships were amazing for me and gave me a glimpse of a different life, one I was starving for.

I saw my very first movie in a theatre…E.T.!

I began watching television and listening to music. I would sit and laugh my head off at the silly movies I watched for the first time, and oh how I loved the discovery of music!

I never disclosed my deep dark secrets to those friends, and because of those dark secrets, I sabotaged the possibilities of romance, because I was absolutely paranoid that I would be discovered.

By now I was 24 years old.

Still living at home.

Still trapped in my own personal hell.

Still hiding the truth.

Still sexually, mentally, emotionally and physically assaulted and abused regularly.

Only it was worse than ever before. The facade was extremely burdensome. I was devoid of self-esteem.

The inward promptings were calling to me, in practically every aspect of my life. I knew I could not continue down this road, but I did not know quite what to do about it.

But at last, I was awakening to possibilities.

The problem was that the more I rejected my father, the angrier and if you can imagine, meaner, he became.

Now, it was combined with death threats towards me and unbelievably, my mother and siblings.

So began a roller coaster of steps forward and steps backwards trying to break free.

Slowly the friendships I had cultivated started changing as the other young people began marrying and having families. I felt left out.

It was my own fault, I could never "get there" with the fine young men who found me attractive and interesting, and missed out on a world of possibilities, and maybe even love!

Finally, I made a huge decision. It was my first in the many forays into self discovery and listening to my heart.

*Chapter 20*

# The Beginnings of Change

The changes were not immediate. They did however, happen. I stumbled and failed. I kept getting back up, sometimes stronger, sometimes weaker, eternally confused, but incredibly desperate to break free.

I've so messed up on my road to self discovery, but over time I made it!

> *"When you're in the middle of a story, it isn't a story at all, but only a confusion; a dark roaring, a blindness, a wreckage of broken glass and splintered wood; like a house in a whirlwind, or else a boat crushed by the icebergs or swept over the rapids, and all aboard powerless to stop it. It's only afterwards that it becomes anything like a story at all. When you are telling it, to yourself or someone else."*

Margaret Atwood, Alias Grace

My first change was to leave the witness religion. I did not feel it had served me. I hated all the requirements, the preaching…the endless laws and more than anything, I hated the hypocrisy. The Bible says, "Thou shall not commit adultery," or lie or a multitude of other things that was contrary to my experience.

I certainly was not prepared for the massive repercussions of that decision. But I just could not ignore the rumblings of my heart.

The knowingness that it was not my calling, that all of this was dead wrong.

Based on the bulk of what I had experienced within that religion, I made the change.

Remember, the tactics of the religion was disfellowshipping its' wayward members. All were to abide by the rules, to never associate with these individuals as a measure to "shake" them into repentance. Also, "bad associations spoil useful habits."

Outside of the religion, I had no friends. I certainly was not prepared for the aftermath of my decision. I was suddenly alone, not a friend in the world. All the people I knew for so many years; suddenly would not speak to me! Even the ones I had considered my best friends.

I knew nobody, outside of my family. Then, my brother disowned me…and abruptly moved himself and his family to California. I would not see him again for 14 years.

During that dark time, I felt that while I had been taught by the witnesses that God was love, then, if this was the kind of love that God represented…I wanted no part of God, or a multitude of other things.

Look what I had experienced at the hands of a "religious" father!

I was lost, abysmally lost. However, this first huge step served as the precursor for other decisions that would eventually be made.

I would go to a restaurant in that little town, and would not get waited on, because the waitress was a witness.

I would go to the bank, wait in line, and upon getting to the counter, the clerk would disappear…she too was a witness.

I know that if I was in an accident on the road, I would not be helped.

For years, the witness people would drive up to my driveway and point and talk. The upside? They didn't come knocking at my door!

I knew I had made a first very good decision for myself, a first of many changes that were to come.

But it certainly was not easy!

# Chapter 21

# Dating and Marriage

Now, comes the next phase of my life as I began to successfully push my father away. He HATED it, and continued to make life miserable.

He and my mom decided to also leave the religion as well. He had come to be disenchanted with it, as he had all the other religions. Besides, I think he realized that he had to accept the inevitable...that I wanted to be married and have my children. His children were leaving the bonds of his control.

I had never dated before...ever! I was now nearly 26 years old.

I knew no single men...I basically knew no one other than a few neighbors.

So I searched the singles columns. The singles columns were far different for the dating sites that we know today. There were little local magazines that had listing after listing of "available" men.

I met a fair share of really creepy men...most of whom made it clear that sex was expected on the first date.

What had I got myself into? I was totally out of my league, completely inexperienced with dating, and I was not a teenager!

Despite my paranoia, I was optimistic that somehow I would get it right. Somehow I would find someone I could love.

Slowly I was waking up.

But…

My secrets had to be kept.

I did my level best to make every appearance of normal. I was incredibly naive!

Eventually, I did meet the man who was to become the father of my two daughters. After a very short period of dating, we married.

Sadly, what I did not understand at that time, is that we attract what we know and are accustomed to!

I had not yet progressed enough to know this. I did not understand the complexities of the man I had attracted into my life.

He came with a ton of baggage. He was an unhappy soul, but I naively thought that given enough time, I could make him happy.

He had recently moved to Arizona from Hawaii, so was establishing himself in a new area with a new job and had no friends locally. I still had only a small friend base.

Our wedding was held at his home, with his folks and uncle, my parents, Karen and a couple who lived next door to me…and his past girlfriend of 10 years.

I did not even know she had been invited…she cried through the entire ceremony, officiated by the local Justice of Peace.

Shortly after we married, we decided to purchase the house my brother and his wife left empty after they had abruptly left for California.

It was next door to my parent's house and the business.

The plan was that my husband and father were going to join forces in the family business with him doing the sales.

This home was one of the oldest homes in this little community. It was tiny home, built poorly, but it became our home. Our plan was to add on and remodel as we went. The inside walls were half thin wood, the top half was cardboard that had been wallpapered. Ripping off the old wallpaper we even found German swastikas!

We knew we had a lot of work ahead, but we felt we could work at it a little at a time. It was something we could afford, the rest could come later.

We were married just shy of three unhappy and miserable years. He thought nudity was beautiful, and I had never been exposed to this and it was difficult for me to understand. He let me know that this was a lifestyle he wanted his family to live. I wasn't game. I associated it with the less savory things I had already experienced in my life.

We took off one Friday afternoon to go camping, shortly after our first daughter was born. We did not arrive at the campground till well after dark. When I awoke early the next morning needing to use the restroom, I was shocked as I stepped out of the tent to see two men walk by…totally nude. Hmm…well it's early?

Ha! It was a nudist camp. If my husband had pre-warned and prepared me for this, perhaps I would have not been so enraged at him…but for me it cast more shadows on our relationship.

There was a lot that transpired during that short three years. My husband and father working together in business was certainly not working. The friction was thick.

My father began trying an all out effort to once again possess. While, I successfully kept him at bay, I foolishly had thought that those years were behind me.

I was always on pins and needles, hiding this fact from my husband, thinking he would not understand, and it would end our marriage. I did not tell him about it before we married, thinking I would NEVER get married!

How my husband did not pick up on things is beyond me…maybe it was all the head butting going on.

Then, something happened that changed everything. Something that resulted in my no longer being willing to tough out the rough spots in our marriage and make it work. I had always known that marriage was work, but this was what I was trying to escape and I would not tolerate this!

Our first daughter was thirteen months old and I was pregnant with our second, just entering my sixth month. We had friends over for dinner, and I left the room to take care of our baby.

When I walked back into the room, my husband was carrying on a conversation with our friends. He hadn't seen me walk into the room. And here he was sharing how he was having an affair with an old girlfriend.

I nearly died on the spot. I abruptly asked our friends to leave. He still had not figured out that I had overheard the conversation. He thought I was nuts, and was not happy with me, as dinner was about to be served.

Once they had left, I explained that I had overheard the conversation…then demanded he leave…NOW! It was happening again…first my father, now my husband.

Leave, he did. He took every piece of furniture in the house, except the crib, an old T.V. and the refrigerator. I had $14 in my purse that I am certain he did not know that I had, or he would have taken it too. He closed down the bank accounts so I had no access to anything.

He refused to pay the debts we had in common, and the debts he had brought into the marriage. The day I had our second daughter, I was served bankruptcy papers.

From the day he left, until after our second baby daughter was born, I never saw nor heard from him. I filed for divorce, and as it turned out the court date was set for June 9th. Our baby was born 2 weeks late, on June 6th. I was not in any kind of shape for a divorce hearing!

But there I was, sitting in the hallway of the courthouse waiting almost an hour and a half to be called in, him sitting right next to me… never asking about the child we had just, obviously had.

When we were called before the judge for our hearing, my husband stated he wanted joint custody. Do NOT let a woman who has just had a baby 3 days prior, be put in that position! I wasn't quite in control of my emotions when I told the judge that while I was obviously no longer pregnant, this man had no idea what we had.

Was it a boy or girl? Was it born alive or dead? What the baby healthy? The judge did not grant the divorce at that time, saying we had issues to iron out. Fortunately the judge was very kind to me, and treated me respectfully.

I filed again when he refused to get counseling, and he did not bother to show up for the hearing, so the divorce was granted a month later.

Ironically, my now ex-husband still did not ask about the sex or wellbeing of his second child until some three months later, when he phoned to ask if he could come see his children.

Welcome to the world of single parenthood!

Yet again, I had allowed myself to be a victim. I did not yet understand the strength I had within.

# Chapter 22

## Making a Living

Three weeks after I had my second baby, my father sat me down and asked me what I intended to do to support my family. At this point I wasn't quite sure, but I was sure I would figure it out. After all I had my special occasion floral business and while I was still growing it, I was sure I could both raise my little family and run my business.

He asked me how much of an idiot loser was I to think I could pull such an insane impossibility. He went off in a tirade of what an imbecile I was, and how I would NEVER make it on my own.

The truth of the matter was that my brother and he had parted ways, and he was really struggling to keep the business going. An even bigger truth is that he really did not want to work any longer.

I knew that the business had been doing really well and was quite a money maker. Problem was, I had never set foot into the sharpening shop and did not know the difference between a router bit and a miter saw!

While I wasn't buying the "I was an idiot" theory he was pounding me with, I was smart enough to understand the benefits of a well-established business, and what it could do for me in raising a family alone. I fully knew that the chance of getting child support was slim to none.

His promise to me was that if I learned the business, it would be mine. That shop was full of noisy big machines, a different one for every kind of tool that needed to be sharpened.

The shop had no air conditioning, and a tin roof, so during the Arizona summer it was beyond miserable. During the winter, it was heated by a wood stove.

My vision of "being trained" for the take-over, was quite different from his. On my first day, he handed me a 4 inch thick notebook which was the instruction manual for a series of three machines that were used for sharpening handsaws. He said that if I could learn these machines by following the instruction manuals, he would consider teaching me the rest.

While I was pretty much blown away, I was determined, despite buckets of tears, and while I destroyed at least 20 handsaws, I slowly started catching on. This trio had a retoothing machine (if a handsaw was too dull, it would be set on a ratchet holder, and run through the machine as it put on an entire new set of teeth). Then it needed to be sent through the setter, to alternate the teeth from left to right, so that it would cut properly. Once set, it needed to be sharpened. He did keep his word, and trained me on the other machines. He was a difficult task master. Seldom praising, always critical and berating, but learn, I did!

It was due to sheer will, grit and determination.

Years later, as I became well established in this industry and met saw sharpeners from all over the country, the story was always the same…sharpening handsaws was one of the hardest skill sets in the business to learn.

My main focus was the steel and aluminum industries, as well as tools for the farmers in the area.

I became known all around the country for my top notch sharpening skills and that business certainly did provide very well for my family for the many years I owned that business. I still own one small segment of that business, and for what little I do with it, it still is a great source of income.

# Chapter 23

## Raising my Family

I loved being a Mom! Motherhood, for me, was what I was cut out for. While at times it was difficult being a single mom, I was happy and grateful to have my children.

My daughters are as different as night and day. My oldest, Lydia was timid, shy and quiet. She would not even attempt to walk till she was sure she would not fall. She knew she was beautiful from the day she was born. I've always called her my beautiful princess.

My second daughter, Jenny, was a tomboy from the start, rough and tumble always coming inside cut and bruised from her daredevil stunts. She also was my chatterbox. She was a much sturdier build than her sister, but just as beautiful. I've always considered her my Egyptian Goddess.

When Lydia was five, I was concerned that she was not emotionally ready for school. I decided to home school for kindergarten only, thinking it would give her a chance to develop more confidence. My business was going well enough that I felt I could spend a half a day teaching her, and a half a day working. My mom volunteered to take care of my girls in the afternoons.

I set up our little schoolroom, and took in another little girl that was five, that we often babysat anyway. Jenny joined us, but I did not focus on her schooling, she was content with the busy work I gave her to do while I worked with the other two girls.

We loved this time! It was fun, and we did some many cool things together that year. The next year rolled around, and I decided to home school just one more year.

What a surprise! I started Jenny out with kindergarten stuff and she was disappointed and bored! I quickly figured out that she had been a little sponge that first year. She had taken it all in and wanted to learn more. So, I included her along with her sister, in first grade learning.

I was fascinated by how differently they learned. Jenny loved to read, devouring every book she could get her hands on…and tell me verbatim what she learned.

Lydia was, on the other hand a kinetic learner. She learned quickly and easily, not by reading, but by building and creating. So for her, we built and created! We built our math equations, we learned almost everything this way and as we did, her confidence grew.

Lydia is the artist in the family. She can cook a meal that is too scrumptious to resist and serve it as an artistic masterpiece. She can paint, she was way more accomplished at the piano and dancing. She was in beauty contests and was crowned Miss (the name of our town) for two years running. She is now a hair artist at a local salon and has quite a large clientele.

Jenny, on the other hand was my scholar. She loved horses, was on the high school swim team and became a swim instructor. She was graduating Phi Theta Kappa from our local community college with her associates degree, when she was just 17.

We enjoyed homeschooling so much that we continued on, the next and the next…and the next till we finished high school…when they were 14 and 15!

It was crazy when the day before Jenny was to graduate from community college, she was informed that she could not graduate, because she did not have her GED! So in order to graduate she had to take the GED the day of her graduation, which she did. She went on to the University of Arizona for a degree in psychology.

She now works at a cancer center with quite a team of people under her leadership.

Those years were, as far as our homeschooling experience… amazing and the glue that kept us through some otherwise very trying times.

We found a home school support group, and formed great friendships. We went on incredible field trips together and worked on learning projects together.

We always had a house full of kids, as they practiced plays and skits. We learned square dancing and all kinds of other fun. We had swim parties, sleepovers and in general some really cool times.

In the meantime, my daughters also had weekly piano lessons, dance lessons, art lessons, horseback riding lessons and a world of amazing experiences I never even dreamed to experience when I was a kid.

They performed in many piano recitals, and I spent a fortune in dance costumes for all the dance recitals they were in.

Because we were home schooling we had opportunities to explore and even travel throughout the year. We typically went camping out on the desert every February. Two weeks, away from the grind (literally) and we had a blast!

One year, our piano teacher was not very happy with me for keeping our camping plans because we had a piano recital coming up a week after our return. I had just purchased another piano for them to replace the very old upright we had…and had not sold it yet. So we loaded the old piano onto a trailer and off we went.

They would spend time every day sitting on the trailer playing the piano…serenading me to the tunes of Chopin, Beethoven and Bach.

On the weekend when friends joined us, we enjoyed their rehearsals as well as the songs we sang around the campfire. All the little dessert creatures enjoyed it as well. It was a time we will never forget.

One of the things I did learn from my father was to be self-sufficient. He had taught all of us kids to be self-sufficient. He taught us construction skills, plumbing skills, landscaping skills, along with the house painting skills with the family business. Before we could learn to drive, we had to know how to change the oil, change and rotate tires, and learn on a stick shift automobile.

I valued those skills, knowing that they were now serving me very well. I chose to impart those skills to my daughters, ensuring that it will serve them well in the future.

So that old home we lived in, became our laboratory. Us girls tore out the old walls and built new walls. We added on. We hung drywall, painted. We added new siding on the outside. We learned some plumbing skills together.

They also learned to sew and cook, and lots of crafts. They helped me in the sharpening business, and each had chores to do to keep the yard and home clean and safe.

I'm not so sure that my daughters always appreciated these valuable life lessons. They have since told me how glad they were that they know what they know and can take care of themselves. They are a bit amazed that many of the young men that they have met do not have any idea how to take care of a home.

# Chapter 24

## The Flip Side of the Coin

The years raising my daughters were also difficult years. Business wise, I excelled and did very well. Schooling, we thrived.

Their father sporadically visited his daughters, but it never really felt like he was there to build a bond for them as much as it was to cause trouble.

For several years, I was in and out of court with accusation after accusation almost every month. Sometimes it was simply over child support. The judge had ordered him to pay quite a monthly sum, but I never saw it.

For the first year after I had Jenny, I was on welfare, so that I could provide while I was learning the business. Welfare kept tabs on the lack of support, which I suspect is what kept the battle going well after I had discontinued the assistance.

Finally, through his pleadings he got child support reduced to $226 per month, which is not much considering I was a full-time parent.

At one point, he demanded through the courts that he get unsupervised visitation. The judge granted it, but every weekend that the girls went with him, they would come back crying and upset. They wouldn't sleep in their own beds for several days after returning home. I had no idea what to think as to why. They were too little to tell me anything that would give me a clue. I just knew that something was not right, and that it was quite the task to get them calmed down again.

One Saturday morning he came to get them, and informed me that he was taking them camping with his new girlfriend. I asked him to sit down so we could talk. He did not want to talk, but finally obliged. I expressed my concern over the emotional state of my daughters each time they returned from his place. I asked him to explain his perspective.

I felt that it was my responsibility as a parent, the full-time caregiver of the girls and the one they looked to for protection that I needed to know. He felt I did NOT need to know, it was none of my business. Not satisfied with that answer, I told them that until he could explain why they were, week after week, returning to me so upset, he would not be taking them with him…particularly this weekend on a camping trip with a brand new girlfriend!

He stormed out the door, slamming it so hard I was amazed the windows did not break!

I did not hear from him again till months later, when I was served papers to appear in court…this time with the accusation that I had pulled a gun on him and threatened to kill him.

I had been in court so many times before over so many supposed issues…I decided I could not bear to go to court one more time! I was done with the nonsense. I was served an arrest warrant on Christmas Eve…for failure to appear.

And then…nothing happened! I did nothing. I heard nothing. And we never saw nor heard from him again. The last time he saw his daughters they were 4 and 5.

Years later, when I decided to visit a young friend in prison, I found out that the warrant for my arrest was still active! I was ordered to go before a judge. He heard my case, and voided the warrant. "You are free to go, we have much bigger fish to fry than to deal with an issue such as this." Needless to say, I was more than relieved! And to think that I had, (likely because of other issues), not given any thought to that outstanding arrest warrant…and if I had been stopped for even a traffic violation, I could have landed in jail.

*Ahh, another angel had my back!*

# Chapter 25

# The Flip Side of Another Coin

Meanwhile, the situation with my father was tenuous at best. He was increasingly becoming more hostile. He drank excessively. If it wasn't his really good homemade beer, which is where his day began, it would finish with many 3 fingers of gin each day.

I was becoming stronger. I was getting better at avoidance and dodging him. I was getting better at responding firmly in rebuttal to his mind-blowing verbal attacks. But this does not mean that I always escaped his vicious tongue and abusiveness.

I had begun getting counseling. I attended a week long retreat on "The Power of the Mind." I read as many books as I could on mindset and gaining inner strength. My heart and mind was beginning to "get" it. I was opened to the fact that I had buried deep inside of me, a strength that I had long since thought I had lost. I had lost before the age of five.

Now, when I saw the abuse that my father was heaping upon my mother, I would stop him. At first it stunned the socks off him. He certainly did not like it.

When he started in on me, I would nip it in the bud. He was shocked. He certainly did not like it. More often than I care to relate, he would fly into a rage unlike any I had seen before. There were threats to kill. He would kill me, he would kill my daughters, he would kill my mom. There were threats that he would end his life. I fully believed those threats. His constant threat was that if I dared to think that I could disappear with my children, he would find and kill us all. I had no doubt.

Yet, he knew I was serious. He knew I was changing. One day, on his flip-sided alter personality type of days, the days when he could be charming and kind, he looked at me and said something profound. He said: "Becky, you have broken the pattern of our family history." I asked him what he meant. He said, "You do not beat your children. You protect them and keep them safe. There is no abusiveness in your blood. You've broken the cycle, and I am proud of you!"

Yes, I was becoming stronger! He recognized it!

By now, I am sure that you are aware I have left out a good portion of the details of this story. I believe that I have given enough of the picture of what my life experiences have been.

# Chapter 26

## It Happened

*I* seldom dated during those years of raising my children. To tell the truth, I really would have loved to have a good man in my life. I just was not so sure that I could find someone right for me, more so, someone who would love me despite my past...and I had enough on my plate.

I ran the family business. I provided well for myself and my children. I home schooled. I also paid off my home, and my parent's home. I paid for their cars and mine. Once I had learned the business, my father had not worked another day in his life. He often just sat outside on his patio, brooding.

When he was not brooding, he was engrossed in building a huge bomb shelter. He felt that America was doomed and he subscribed to the teachings and the underground movements of the militia. The bomb shelter was filled with guns of all kinds, even illegal ones. It was filled with food and water, composting toilets...and it contained the means by which the inhabitants of the shelter could quickly and easily take their lives if need be. There were gas masks, special glasses in case of nuclear war...He purchased all of this from the income I made from the sharpening business.

Yes, he and my mother handled only the money part of the business. I made so much during those years, and that money funded all his projects…but I had no control of the money…except to receive a pay check. I did ALL the work…including deliveries. While I was paid well, I soon tired of this game. It would result in an increase of pay, but not full control…uhm, I thought this business was turned over to me? I thought you said it would be mine!

The business was free and clear. I paid for so much more than I have time and space to tell about. I worked hard and I was always exhausted.

I started dating a man that I wanted to get to know better. We had not dated long when we decided all of us would go to my sister and brother in law's home to celebrate my Lydia's 10th birthday. We spent a day celebrating a beautiful young girl close to becoming a young lady. On the second morning, we all decided to go for a short hike. My sister and her husband lived in a beautiful rural setting in southern Arizona.

February in Arizona is beautiful. The day was gorgeous. As we meandered along enjoying the hike, Tim and I lagged behind about 20 feet. We were simply talking and getting to know each other. My girls and nephew ran back and forth between Tim and I and the others. It was a good time.

As we returned to my sister's home, suddenly my father went into a boiling rage. He screamed at me in front of my children, my new boyfriend, my sister and brother in law…"How could you behave in such a manner!!! How could you possibly think that having sex with this man in front of all of us is right? How could you behave so despicably? In front of your children, Becky!"

Everyone was stunned in disbelief. My children were crying in confusion and fear. Me? I was incensed, almost beyond control. I ordered everyone to get their belongings and get in the car NOW.

I refused to let my father drive. No one spoke on the long drive home. I drove in stony silence. I was done.

When we arrived home, I told my parents to GO home. I told Tim to go home. He kept asking me to tell him what on earth this was about. I told him I would, but not now, and insisted he leave, promising to call him in the morning.

I spent the rest of the afternoon quietly contemplating every avenue of the course of action I should take. I had my daughters go to bed early. They too were upset and did not understand what happened.

After they were asleep, I walked to my parent's home. Of course my father was sitting in his patio. I walked up to him and said, "This is over. Tomorrow morning, you will take the camp trailer, the jeep, and whatever belongings you wish to take and you will go. You will go, and you will NEVER return. You will go and you will find your own happiness. You will never again set foot on this property. I will not leave. I have worked hard for this business that is now mine, but you continue to control. I have personally paid for everything…this house, my house, the trailer and jeep you will be taking. Everything. You just cannot be happy here, no matter how hard we have all tried. We've each taken your abuse for far longer than should ever have been allowed to happen…to no avail. It hasn't mattered. None of us can ever make you happy. Only YOU can make you happy and it is time you learn this. This is over, and do not think for one minute that I am kidding. If you do not leave in the morning, I will call the authorities and have you removed. So, I suggest you comply. I wish you well."

Then, I turned around and walked away.

In the morning, I started school for my daughters, trying to keep some kind of semblance of order. It was impossible. I kept watching for my father to come by and get the camp trailer. He didn't.

I called Tim, explained briefly what had happened and asked him to meet me at my parents.

I gave my daughters some assignments and walked again to my parent's house. He was still in bed. It was 10 a.m. and he was typically an early riser.

I walked into the house, past my mother, and into his bedroom. I told him to get up, get dressed, and get going. NOW! I knew I could not back down. I knew I would not back down.

He did get up. He did get dressed. He did not pack. He did not load up the camp trailer.

Tim arrived. My father stomped around. He was livid. He demanded to see my daughters. He said he wanted to tell them goodbye.

I called for them to come over to their grandparents.

When they arrived, we were all standing on the walkway of their driveway. He had his gun with him, which was not unusual…he always had a gun on him. He had packed nothing.

He first hugged Lydia, then Jenny and told them he loved them and he was sorry he had to say goodbye. Lydia started crying, begging him not to go.

He next walked up to me. He grabbed my face, pressing hard. He demanded I kiss him goodbye. I refused. He walked up to my mother put his hand on her shoulder and shoved her, hard. Then he walked up to Tim. He reached his arm back to take a swing at Tim. Tim caught him by surprise, grabbing his arm and yelled: "No hold it! You can hit me. Go ahead take a swing. You better make it good. But stand forewarned, if you hit me, I will cream you. I will lay you flat. Do you really want that?"

With that, my father dropped his arm, walked out to the jeep, got in and drove away.

While none of us knew what lay before us, I think we all had a sense of what would happen. In my heart, I knew there was a good chance he would make good his threat…or threats.

Tim and I sat down and talked. I apologized that this had happened. He made it clear that he was washing his hands of the situation. He left, and I never saw nor heard from him again, and I did not blame him.

*Another angel sent to help!*

# Chapter 27

# The Aftermath

By the next morning, he had not returned. I knew it was best to go to the authorities to file a missing person report. I was trembling. I explained that I had no idea where he went. I expected he may have taken his life, but that because of his meanness he could well be alive, and our lives could be in serious danger.

I knew that if he was alive, he had always said that we were to NEVER go to the authorities in regards to anything pertaining to him, and made clear what the repercussions would be.

I insisted that we would need extra protection and possibly to be given new identities somewhere far away. They agreed to go by my wishes, both with new identities if need be, and the missing person report not be announced on the news.

My father's friends searched everywhere. Law enforcement searched. Friends across the country were notified. We started getting reports of him being seen both locally and in other states.

Meanwhile, three days into this long ordeal of not knowingness, my mother looked at me and asked: "Your father molested you didn't he?" I looked at her and asked: "You knew?" "Yes, I've known for a long time," she answered quietly.

I will leave this without saying more.

After two long weeks had passed, the Sheriff came to me and said, "Becky, it is time. We have to put this out to the press. We will provide the protection you need, as promised, but we cannot let this go on any longer."

I agreed…reluctantly. It was on the news Monday morning. That year had been quite rainy, making it impossible to travel many of the back desert roads. But the weekend before the press released the information was a gorgeous sunny weekend. Hikers and 4 wheeling enthusiasts took to the desert to enjoy the beauty.

It only took minutes after the announcement when several calls came through saying they had seen a jeep that matched the description way out on the desert some 50 miles west of our homes.

The Sheriff and my father's friends took off to follow the leads they had received.

They discovered his body, estimated time of death, two weeks prior.

He left a note in the jeep: "Thanks for a good life."

We were not allowed to identify the body, for good reasons, but not identifying his body played games on our heads for many years.

# Chapter 28

## Deep Dark Secrets in Abundance

I had felt for many years, even as a youth, that I was somehow instrumental in keeping us all alive. I deeply felt that it was my own strength that kept any kind of life going. Perhaps it was misguided. Perhaps it came from by being made the caregiver for the family at the age of eight. I felt that if I took the toughest and most consistent abuse, it would soften things for the rest.

I am the first to say, I wish I had had the strength, the wisdom and the courage to leave forever, before I was five, or for that matter, any time thereafter. If I had managed to find my way the first time, perhaps I would have suffered a worse fate if some unsavory person had picked up off the streets of L.A. all those years ago. I do not know and never will.

If I had a dollar for every time I THOUGHT about leaving, but did not follow through because I was brain frozen, paralyzed by fear and did not know how, I would truly be wealthy. Maybe I would have spared all of us from what we each went through. Maybe, it would have shaken my father awake? I do not know and never will know…but you know what?

My past is full of maybes and regrets, but it does not pay to look back and dwell there. I learned that the activity of worrying about the past kept me immobilized and victimized, without the ability to be a force for the change I want to see in our world. I have no excuses. What happened to me is what has made me who I am today. While I am NOT proud of what happened, I simply cannot change it, and daily I strive to rise above it.

*"We aren't the weeds in the crack of life. We're the strong, amazing flowers that found a way to grow in the most challenging conditions."*

–Jeanne McElvaney, Spirit Unbroken: Abby's Story

After his death, we came together as a family. All except the youngest, Sharon was present. As the kids played, the adults talked.

I brought up my own personal dark secret. It opened the doors for admissions from the others.

Each had been sexually abused, even my brother, even my sister in law. For each, the sexual abuse happened, but not as extensively as it had happened to me. But it happened. None of us had known the other had experienced this. None of us had confided in each other. None of us had dared seek help from outside sources.

We had all been told and believed that we and each other would be killed if we told. Did Sharon escape this or was that at the root of her rebellion? We do not know.

We all acknowledged the other kinds of abuse that we had experienced…and how that too had affected us.

It was a very tough conversation to have, but quite an eye opener.

Because of the dynamics, I was fearful that our children would hear about our experiences, either from a healing family member, or otherwise.

On a side note, we were beginning to be exposed to the fact that my father's indiscretions extended far beyond our immediate family.

I suggested that our children who ranged between 9 and 16 should hear about this from the source. I did not want them hearing from someone else. As painful as it was, they needed to hear from us, not an outsider…or even risk the chance of one of the youngsters overhearing it from one of us adults and not getting the full story. After hours of discussion, we all agreed.

It was so difficult to relate our story to our children. It was scary and heart wrenching to watch our kids take this information in and process it.

Was it the right decision? We believe it was. Did this bring extended issues that needed to be addressed? Very much so. But I continue to feel that the decision made was the wisest we could have made.

*Musings: In the writing of this story, I no longer have to live with secrets! It is done. If, by the telling of this story, I affect positively even one person…then it is worth the hours and the tears spent writing.*

Forgiveness, even of myself, does not change the past, *but it makes the future infinitely brighter!*

The greatest gift we can give to ourselves is to love ourselves.

The greatest gift we can give our family is to love ourselves.

The greatest gift we can give the world is to love ourselves.

Because, unless and until we do…how do we expect to let our light shine in this world for all to see? And how do we live with the memories? How do we become whole for perhaps the first time in our lives?

*Musings: It certainly takes more courage and strength to walk away from a bad situation than to stay in it. Staying is familiar, no matter how bad it is, you kind of know what you are up against. To leave means stepping into the unknown and uncharted waters.*

*Chapter 29*

# *New Beginnings and Healing*

*Musings: "There is no greater threat to the critics and cynics and fear mongers than those of us who are willing to fall, because we have learned how to rise."*

The quote above and the following comes from Brené Brown's book; Rising Strong - The Reckoning, The Rumble, The Revolution

*"Understanding and Combating Shame: Shame derives its power from being unspeakable. That's why it loves perfectionists...we're so easy to keep quiet. If we cultivate enough awareness about shame to name it and speak to it, we've basically cut it off at the knees. Just the way exposure to light was deadly for the Gremlins, language and story bring light to shame and destroy it."*

*"Character is formed by the willingness to accept responsibility for one's own life, it is the source from where self respect springs."*

Joan Didion

The road to recovery for our family has been a long and ongoing one. Sometimes issues, pop to the surface when least expected.

For me, at the oddest moments, something happens that triggers deep seated emotions that I thought was resolved.

On my own journey to healing, I have read some remarkable books written by incredible people. One of the coolest things I have read, at the onset of my "awakening" gave me so much to ponder.

*"Our deepest fear is not that we are inadequate.*

*Our deepest fear is that we are powerful beyond measure. It is our light, not our darkness that most frightens us.*

*We ask ourselves, 'Who am I to be brilliant, gorgeous, talented, fabulous?' Actually, who are you not to be? You are a child of God.*

*Your playing small does not serve the world. There is nothing enlightened about shrinking so that other people won't feel insecure around you.*

*We are all meant to shine, as children do. We were born to make manifest the glory of God that is within us.*

*It's not just in some of us; it's in everyone. And as we let our own light shine, we unconsciously give other people permission to do the same. As we are liberated from our own fear, our presence automatically liberates others."*

– Marianne Williamson

# Chapter 30

# My Own Little Family

*"Nobody knew she carried a secret universe in her heart, but those brave enough to enter that space and see what a beautiful galaxy her love could be."*

Mark Anthony

Thankfully, time is a healer. It does not mean that it is all easy. My daughters grew up and were going their own directions, to work and college. My home was empty. I was accustomed to it being the gathering place for all the young people in our lives, and I missed them and those times so much.

Finally, I decided it was my time. I went to Los Angeles to a class called "How to Catch a Guy and Keep Him." Sitting in the packed audience, I observed an audience full of women, many of whom were fresh out of broken relationships and they were still unsettled and angry.

I realized I had been working on myself for some time…and that I was no longer angry. I felt that now I could enter the dating scene. The class gave an informative session on online dating, which I had tried previously, and met a fair share of unsuitable, for me, males. I decided to give it another shot, so started with match.com.

First though, I read through the listings of available prospects and quickly discovered that none of these individuals struck my interest. Then I read one that did.

I loved what he had written, so posted my own bio. He saw my bio and contacted me! We met on Dec. 28th 2006 and married ten months later.

He is the most peaceful, kindest, truest, loving man I could have ever dreamed of meeting, and has in every way been a huge factor in my healing.

I've been so very blessed by him. When we first started dating, he always told me how I often screamed out and cried in my sleep at night. He was concerned, but patient and loving. I no longer do that.

I have always been brutally honest with him as to what he was taking on, so there have been no real surprises for him, of "why didn't you tell me about this?," except for the things that I simply could not remember, that have been brought back because of something that triggered an emotion and activated a memory.

With him, have come his three wonderful grown children and seven of our eight grandchildren, his parents and siblings.

*"Healing comes from gathering wisdom from past actions and letting go of the pain that the education cost you."*

–Caroline Myss

# Chapter 31

# My Mom

In the beginning, we were all pretty messed up. My mom and I fought over everything. I was angry with her, she was angry with me. I really struggled with the fact that she had known. She was struggling too.

I am such a mama bear when it comes to my own children…how could a mother let this happen? I finally have had to accept that she too was a victim and I simply must let it go.

She was such a mess that she begged constantly for one or the other of my daughters to stay the night with her, as she could not bear to be alone. I conceded for awhile, till I had mutiny on my plate with my daughters protesting.

She and I, on one occasion came to blows with each other. I am not proud to say it, but it did get excessively explosive. It shook both of us deeply, and I plunged into a depression. I had never hit anyone in my life! For both of us, it was culmination of all those years of keeping quiet, the pent up anger and the feelings of betrayal.

We pretty much avoided each other as much as possible for some time after that.

She had never worked. There was a good many things she had never done before. She had never pumped gasoline for her own car.

I swear she picked up guys, simply by standing at the gas pump crying because she did not how to pump her own gas! The first time yes, perhaps I get that, but time after time?

Then she looked up a childhood friend who was recently widowed. That did it...she moved away to Nevada with him and several years later they married. I believe the separation, living away from each other was the best thing that could happen. While we stayed in touch, there was a whole lot we each needed to work through. It helped both of us to have our own time and space to grow and heal on our own.

My daughters and I surprised her by showing up just in time for their wedding.

This man had recently lost his wife to cancer, a daughter who was born with serious birth defects and his mother all in one year. I do not believe he had a clue what he was getting himself into! Fortunately, they've worked things out though and are still married today.

I fully realize that each one of us has to process in our own way. Each of us individually has had huge choices and decisions to make. We also need to remember that if we do not agree with another's way of coping and dealing, it is not our life to live. It is theirs. It is however, our responsibility to act with love, caring, concern and a non judgmental attitude.

# Chapter 32

# My Brother

Meanwhile, in the two weeks that my father had gone missing, both of my daughters started their monthly cycles. Was I in for some fun!

If there was ever anything that softened their grandfather, it was these two little girls. He was a different person around them, and for a time it gave hope. He adored them. It did not mean I did not take huge precautions when they were going to be around him. But incredibly, he did adore them.

Very young, I would speak to them about staying close to each other and protecting each other. I also spoke often about what they needed to do should ANY member of the opposite sex, start touching them in ways they should not be touched. We had conversations early in their lives about always telling me and how careful they should be.

I also warned my father that if he even thought about doing anything inappropriate to my daughters, I would kill him. I was ready to go to jail if need be to stop him cold. He knew I meant it. Happily, I can say that he never did lift a hand in any kind of abuse against either of my daughters.

In this part of the story, I will digress a bit, to pull together the picture of the last several years of his life.

My brother and his family decided, after 14 years, to reconnect with our family. By now they had 3 boys, and had lost a daughter to crib death. Their youngest son is 3 months older than my youngest daughter.

It was a time with lots of turmoil and adjusting. There was a lot of back and forth visits from them from California.

They were and still are Jehovah's Witnesses. I am not so sure why the change of heart, except my brother said that he realized that the Bible says that, "You should honor your father and your mother."

Over the period of two years or so, things had changed with his relationship with his wife. He was considering leaving her. He brought 2 of his 3 boys to spend the summer. He stayed in a guest cottage on my parent's property, the boys stayed with my daughters and I. It made for quite an added load of work and challenge.

As it turned out, my brother and father still could not connect and were constantly at odds. Something transpired between the two of them, I do not know what. The boys had already gone to bed, when he knocked on my door asking me to get his boys up and send them over to him immediately. I did. It was a hot summer evening. They got up and walked over to his cottage barefoot and in boxer shorts, no shirts nor shoes. They did not come back.

Turns out, my brother had packed his own belongings, which none of us were aware of, he told the boys he was going to take them for ice cream, but instead got on the road, in the middle of the night headed back to California. The boys had no shirts, nor shoes, and all of their belongings were at my home. I often wonder what they felt to be pulled away in this manner.

My mom got frantic, and tried numerous times to call him…but no answer. Finally, the oldest grandson called a few days later, saying they were back at home, but that he could not talk.

Two months later, we received a letter. It was an "anonymous" letter describing in detail how my brother had died. My mom practically went nuts. Her uncle was visiting at the time, and listened for several hours to the wailing and sadness, when he asked her to give him the telephone. He dialed the number to my brother's place of business in California…guess who answered the phone? And guess who wrote that awful letter?

Unbelievable, and from my perspective on life, this was quite simply another painful form of abuse.

So, what we had hoped for was restored family relationships had dissolved again…until after my father had taken his life.

They came to be with us after my father was found, and while I found it difficult to trust, we were going through some really tough times, so while there is a relationship of sorts, it was never with full giving.

Then, the unspeakable happened again in our family. His second son, who had had issues with bipolar tendencies, had gone into the army despite health conditions. He could not maintain the grind of it all, went AWOL, was in lots of trouble, and at age 21 took his life…just two years after his grandfather had. He was at a military base in Oklahoma, and had simply walked off base. He was found in the mountains, under a tree some 3 months later by a hunter.

My brother and sister in-law, have never been the same since. I am not sure if any of us would be if we had lost two children.

Visiting him recently, I was struck by similarities. A tendency he, my sister, my mom and I all have in common is staying very busy. He works from sun up to sun down, often for no particular reason or need… except perhaps, as an outlet to escape his pain.

There is not one conversation that he does not bring up death or dying. Yes, he is an insurance agent, yes as an agent you deal with a lot of those issues. But he spends so much time dwelling on it that it seems to be his only focus.

He is still a witness, not because it speaks to his soul, but because his oldest son is a witness and yields the power of the decision. Upon asking my brother why he still stays with something that does not resonate with him, he explains that he has no choice. His son would never let him see his granddaughters again if he did not continue in the faith.

My oldest nephew has also disowned his only living sibling, because the youngest has decided that religion is not to his liking. The oldest let him know that his brother's little baby girl would never be a part of his family's life…because of religion.

And so the cycle continues on. To me, it is abuse, plain and simple. And I continue to ask why? Did we not learn?

*Chapter 33*

# My Sister and Brother In-Law

Meanwhile my sister and brother-in-law, decided in the process of their own healing, that none of our family is good enough for them, except for my oldest daughter.

I have chosen to love from a distance, not because that is the way I would wish or prefer it to be, but because I need to protect myself. It is my way to grow, to heal and be the best I can be. Also, I will not take responsibility for the others. I can only deal with and face my own journey.

The last time I was in their home, my brother-in-law said to me: "Becky, I dislike you very much." Why?" I asked in disbelief. "Because you did not protect your sister. You simply stood by and let her be abused."

That was a tough pill to swallow. I replied: *"But, don't you realize that I was only two years older? I could not even protect myself! To this day she still says that I was the only mother she ever had!"* To which he replied "if you were made of anything worth anything, you would have protected her. Since you had not, we really do not care to be around you."

I was stunned, hurt deeply and have only had a "courtesy in their presence" relationship with them since. While I would prefer otherwise and sorely miss my sister, nothing I say or do will change the situation.

*"Forgiveness, quite frankly, is the most selfish thing you can do. Because it is the greatest thing you can do for yourself."*

–Caroline Myss

# The Woman I Love

(written by my husband, Mark)

As Becky mentioned before, we met on December 28, through Match.com. It was both of our first time on a dating site. I also met some real strange people before Becky. I had just changed jobs from Southern California, and I was working third shift at my job, and worked Sundays, so if I was going to meet anyone, I only had Friday and Saturday evenings to do so, because all of the rest of the week I was either working or sleeping. I was new to third shift, and it was not an easy adjustment for me to make. I met a few women in bars, but I was not really a bar person. I have not been religious for many years, so meeting women in a church environment was not going to happen.

So we met on our first date, on a weekday so it was an early evening because I had to go to work straight from the restaurant. But I saw potential in her, and looked forward to our next date, which turned out to be on New Year's Eve. We went to a local mall type place that has several clubs and restaurants. We were having a good time, but it was apparent to both of us that we were not late night party people, so when she asked if we could go to her house to be with her daughter, who was home from college for a long weekend, that was OK with me.

We continued seeing each other, and it was very comfortable. It wasn't too long before she told me about her sharpening business, and she explained that she would be working a long day at the shop. I volunteered to help her, if she thought that I could be of any help.

Needless to say, that day was a hard, long day for both of us, but I think that seeing each other, new to a relationship, work like that for twelve hours to finish everything, made a lasting impression for both of us. For me, seeing her take command of several types of sharpening machines, and coordinate all of the side work, plus train me to do the chores that I was performing, was an eye opener, and I was impressed at her work ethics and ability.

For her, I think she saw in me the ability for me to adapt to something I had never done before, and yet I was right there with her the whole time, and we had only known each other for a few weeks, was just as impressive for her. We ended up having a late dinner together, and our love and respect has only increased and improved since.

Once we started seeing each other full time, we began having the conversations of her past, and it was hard to listen to. At times I remember thinking, wow, it is pretty early in our relationship to admit to some of the things she was telling me, but it was an amazing story of survival, and I never once thought badly, or of leaving because it might be too much baggage. When she would tell me of some of the more graphic things she talks about in this book, I saw in her the hurt in her eyes, and on every occasion, although she never once shed a tear while telling me in detail of the abuse, I knew that I had one strong woman here, and I was sure that we were going to be perfect for each other.

I remember the first time I took her to meet my parents, we met for breakfast in a restaurant. After one meeting, my father pulled me aside, and said "You have met a wonderful lady there, she is a gem" and told me "do not to do anything that might fuck it up, OK?"

Well, I laughed at my father's abruptness, but I will always remember how she impressed my folks during a one hour breakfast meeting.

The years have been filled with ghosts from her past. At first Becky seemed like she was too eager to please, not wanting to make any decisions that might make me feel uncomfortable. Little things like where we went to eat, what movie we would see…those little things. I could tell she was uncomfortable dating, and she admitted she had not dated much in her life, and we were in our late forties!

When we started sleeping together, she would wake me up with her nightmares, and I would always wake her up to end the dream, and I would hold her until she stopped shaking. Those nightmares took several years, but they finally started getting fewer and further between.

I feel what has impressed me the most, is her transformation. Now that I know the whole story, and I did not learn it all from editing her book, I, too see that little girl in her come through, and I have seen it many times, now that I know what to look for.

The little girl comes out in the form of taking time to get her feet wet in a small creek while we are camping, and seeing the look on her face as she sits there on the edge of the creek, bare feet in the water, eyes closed, facing the warm sun, deep in thought.

She comes out when I see her playing little kid games with our grandson; getting just as involved in the game as he is. She has transformed from the helpless victim to a survivor, and there is no doubt in my mind that what she still hides, is a gruesome past, but the light that shines through is one of strength, pride, and modesty, for she is still a victim, healing, living, surviving her horrible past.

It saddens me to hear and see how her sisters still hold her accountable for the abuse that was given them. How could she have possibly stopped the abuse when she was right there getting the blunt of it herself? I realize that some people are stronger than others, and I am proud to say that my wife, although it has taken many years, is the survivor of the family. There seems to be a varying degree of healing, and I hope someday her sisters will see Becky as who she really is, and not the scapegoat they have made her into. Becky has survived some of the most horrible kinds of abuse, and had to deal with it for many years. I am proud of the woman I married, for she has the heart and soul of a true survivor. She is truly, "The Woman I Love" as well!

*Chapter 35*

# Words from my Auntie Elizabeth

"In 2004 I reconnected with my sister and pretty much turned my life upside down. I had been living a quiet, retired life.

One phone call initiated the start of the get reacquainted period with my sister and her family after a 45 year absence. I learned that her first husband had passed away, she was remarried to a childhood friend, and her family had grown from two to four children. I told her all about everything that had transpired in mine over the many decades long separation.

We did our best to resume a sisterly relationship, but sadly, it just wasn't meant to be. We have ceased communication and that is okay. I hope she is happy and enjoying her life.

I am very satisfied that I took a chance and broke the silence. While I do not see my sister, I gained four nieces, a nephew-in-law and an adorable great-great nephew who has completely charmed me.

One of these nieces is the author of this book you are reading and I am so proud of her I could burst.

She endured unspeakable abuse both physical and sexual. She had unrealistic responsibilities heaped on her when she was a very young child. She had to endure change after change in locations and religions and life became very confusing.

She was taken away from grandparents, great-grandparents and an auntie who adored her and her brother.

I honestly do not know how she survived all the horrible events of her life. The key word here is survivor…her will to live and get through each day had to have been so strong.

But, as I said, she is a survivor. Not only did she survive, she thrives. She has owned and operated several successful businesses and is smart as a whip.

She homeschooled her daughters and they inherited their mom's intelligence and resilience. She is kind and caring and knows how to be a friend.

Happily, she met a wonderful man who loves her with all his heart and does all he can to protect her. They have a lovely relationship and that is another miracle as she had no role models to observe.

Another sign of her spirit and resilience is that she now wants to tell her story and lift abuse out of the shadows. I know she believes that if someone has suffered such trauma can come out whole on the other side, then maybe she has found her real purpose.

I believe she can be a resource to women and men and let them know that they too can be whole, that they have reason to hope."

# Chapter 36

## The Woman I Love

From my daughter, Jenny

Before I start, I want to say something about how proud I am of my mom. She has written this incredible, well-written and enlightening book about abuse. Too often, it feels that abuse is a "taboo" topic. Polite society ignored it, family members who suspected, ignored it. It's because they were too afraid to "rock the boat" as my great-grandparents put it. But what would have happened if it HADN'T been ignored? I wonder this all of the time.

I fully admit, this was a hard book for me to read. Its feels like I always knew that abuse had happened, that there was something so horribly, fundamentally wrong with the mercurial man I knew and loved. To me, he was Papa. He would spoil my sister and I horribly, buying boxes of the types of candy bars we loved, and for me, being obsessed with horses, boxed sets of toy horses to placate and encourage that love.

But then, what felt like mere minutes later, he would turn, and what had started out (to me at least) as a wonderful family dinner, would turn into a rant lasting into the wee hours of the morning. I think that is where my obsession with learning came from at that young age. We would be required, each and every one of us, to recite (in our own words,

137

never repeating what someone else had said) what was done that was so wrong, and what we "learned" from this talk.

I still remember the day he left...vividly. I was so angry when he left, because I KNEW what he would do. How could a 9 year old child KNOW that their grandpa would kill himself?

I was angry for a long time, at my Grandma mostly, on behalf of my Mom. I knew what kind of mother my mom was: loving, loyal, hard-working, and above all, protective. How could my Nana *ALLOW* this abuse to happen for so long? My Mom is the one who has helped me to let go of this anger. I still call my grandma weekly, and have a great relationship with her.

I am beyond proud of the strong, incredible woman that my mom found within herself. I can remember the dark days of her depression. The days that even the jokes and stories that my sister and I would tell to try and make her laugh of childhood transgressions, would make her feel that we were laughing at her down-falls as a mother. My mom has come a long way – she can laugh now at our silly stories, and while she does still battle with some of the insecurities, she has learned to "snap" herself out of it.

I know that our family still disappoints her. They disappoint me too. All that my mom has wanted is for our family to come together, be stronger together. Perhaps someday this will till happen. I hope that they read this and come to understand my mother a little better, how I know her. As a survivor. As the strong, wonderful, smart, kind, giving, loving, forgiving and powerful woman that she is. She is, The Woman that I Love!

# Chapter 37

# *Mindset*

While it often difficult to come to love and respect yourself once you have been a victim of abuse, it is imperative. Come out of the darkness and into the light!

*"Do not speak badly of yourself, for the warrior that is inside you hears your words and is lessened by them. You are strong and you are brave. There is a nobility of spirit within you. Let it grow."*

David Gemmell

I have found that as I began to shift my mindset to belief in myself, it is that belief that helped to make the transition.

*"Courage is taking the first steps to your dream even when you can't see the path ahead."*

*"Love yourself through this process and don't be too hard on yourself even when you stumble and fall. It is imperative that we forgive our past self. When we confront the dark parts of ourselves, and work to banish them with the light of forgiveness, our willingness to wrestle with our demons in this way will cause our angels to sing. No matter what has happened it does not mean we are bad, it means we are human...and we need to get really bored*

139

*with our past because it is over. Focus on now and what you will do now to live a joy filled life!"*

http://www.marcandangel.com/2015/05/10/16-simple-ways-to-love-yourself-again/

Writing this book has been a really interesting experience for me. Yes, it has been emotional. It has been healing. I have learned much about how focusing on writing my own story instead of simply reading, hearing and watching everyone else's story has done for me. When I catch myself comparing my life to someone else's, and feeling less than…I remember that people often only show their highlight reel… especially in the public eye. They often do not share their reality.

What we must come to realize is that our greatest task is really about discovering self love…it is about breaking down the gigantic walls we have built around ourselves. When we are courageous enough to love ourselves, to get to know and embrace ourselves despite the past, despite our flaws, despite the rejection and despite abuse and how we did or did not handle the situation, we also open the door to connecting with others who are truly worth loving. Loving ourselves paves the way to healthier, more enriching relationships.

And remember this: You don't have to wait for an apology to forgive. For many of us that will never happen. Life truly does get much easier when you can learn to accept all the apologies you never got.

The key is that realizing the grudges and painful memories from the past are a total waste of today's happiness and holding on to them is like letting unwanted company live rent free in your head.

Forgiveness is a promise to yourself that you want to keep. Forgiving is making a promise not to hold onto the unchangeable past. Forgiveness has everything to do with freeing yourself of the burden of being the eternal victim.

I would like to encourage you to also tell your story…it may be the most powerful medicine in your healing process that you could ever include in your arsenal of healing tips.

Each time you tell your story it keeps you in touch with your purpose in life and those that hear your story it provides connection.

It has been proven that the support you receive by telling your story actually can flip off the toxic stress hormones, and flip on relaxation responses that release healing hormones. Not only does this turn on the body's innate self-repair mechanisms and function as preventative medicine—or treatment if you're sick. It also relaxes your nervous system and helps heal your mind of <u>depression</u>, anxiety, <u>fear</u>, <u>anger</u>, and feelings of disconnection.

As I have written this book, I amazingly have come across other women who have also gone through their own hell with abuse, and who are thriving.

We have formed strong support system for those who have been there and are ready to grow and thrive.

> *"You either get bitter or you get better. It's that simple. You either take what has been dealt to you and allow it to make you a better person or you allow it to tear you down. The choice does not belong to fate. It belongs to you."*

> Josh Shipp

# Chapter 38

# An Invitation

Over four years ago, I began a book publishing company. My company works with aspiring authors assisting and coaching them in the writing, publishing and marketing of their books.

This has been an amazing experience and I really love working with my authors. The wealth of knowledge and experience is inspiring, eye opening and educational. There is not a day that goes by that I do not learn and am impacted positively by the stories, the legacy that these individuals are sharing with the world. Some are showcasing their expertise to grow their business. Others are writing children's stories, fiction books, writing journals and workbooks, even coloring books and more.

Among them are people like myself, who have decided it is time to share their own story.

We offer several different packages:

- Signature Story: This is a story you tell to weave cohesiveness into your WHY you are in the business you are in, and provides a connection with your clients and prospects.

- Journey to Authorship: This is a 12 week live and interactive group training for book writing, publishing and marketing. Includes three private coaching sessions. We provide resources for editing, formatting, book covers and so much more.

- Interview Style Books: This method proves to be an excellent solution for those who struggle with writing. We set up interview sessions that are recorded, then to a transcriptionist. Once the transcription is complete, it is edited and completed, ready for publishing. Many of my clients wanting to tell their story have found this to be powerful option.

### *"We Choose to Thrive: The Amazing Voices of Abuse Victims Telling Their Stories of Healing and Their Choice to Thrive."*

**"We Choose to Thrive"** is a movement of sorts. This is an incredible opportunity for you to be a part of a project that has been recently launched, with the intention of turning into a book series, perhaps even a movie.

Our goal is to make a huge impact on our world. Our ambition is to change/impact a million lives…and one of the ways we intend to do this is by sharing a minimum of 1,000 stories of survival and thriving.

We are collecting stories of women…and men who want to share their story. It is also open to those who love their loved ones and want to share the story of why they love their survivor/thriver.

This will be done in an interview type of story…guidelines will be answering the following questions:

1. Briefly tell us your story
2. Where are you now on your healing path?
3. What has been the most positive thing you have done for yourself to overcome the trauma of your past?
4. What words of wisdom can you offer to those just beginning on their own journey of healing?
5. What resources can you recommend for those who are need of support?

You will be able to submit your story to be added to our upcoming book release by following this link:

http://goo.gl/forms/U3C83rwxwskP7xfl2

Requirements:
* We ask for your name and email address so that we can confirm / ask supplementary questions as need be.
* You have the option to NOT include your name with this story if that is your preference.
* This story will be included both on our blog and in our book.
* It is limited to 2,000 words
* We reserve the right to accept or decline an interview based on our own discretion.
* You will be required to sign a waiver permitting us to publish your story in our book.
* Here is the link to the Google document if you are interested in participating:  http://goo.gl/forms/U3C83rwxwskP7xfl2

I believe that you will know immediately what resonates for you and extend a heartfelt invitation to you to explore what you feel works for you.

# Chapter 39

# Resources and Bibliography

As parents, we need to be ever vigilant to teach our children from the moment they are born to believe in themselves. Words spoken can either build confidence or tear it down. Be vigilant to observing your children and watch for any signs that something is not right.

*"Child abuse is more than bruises and broken bones. While physical abuse might be the most visible, other types of abuse, such as emotional abuse and neglect, also leave deep, lasting scars. The earlier abused children get help, the greater chance they have to heal and break the cycle—rather than perpetuate it. By learning about common signs of abuse and what you can do to intervene, you can make a huge difference in a child's life."*

*"Child sexual abuse is an especially complicated form of abuse because of its layers of* **guilt and shame.** *It's important to recognize that sexual abuse doesn't always involve body contact. Exposing a child to sexual situations or material is sexually abusive, whether or not touching is involved.*

*While news stories of sexual predators are scary, what is even more frightening is that sexual abuse usually occurs at the hands of someone the child knows and should be able to trust—most often close relatives. And contrary to what many believe, it's not just girls who are at risk. Boys and girls both suffer from sexual abuse. In fact, sexual abuse of boys may be underreported due to shame and stigma.*

*Aside from the physical damage that sexual abuse can cause, the* **emotional component is powerful and far-reaching.** *Sexually abused children are tormented by shame and guilt. They may feel that they are responsible for the abuse or somehow brought it upon themselves. This can lead to self-loathing and sexual problems as they grow older—often either excessive promiscuity or an inability to have intimate relations.*

*The shame of sexual abuse makes it very difficult for children to come forward. They may worry that others won't believe them, will be angry with them, or that it will split their family apart. Because of these difficulties, false accusations of sexual abuse are not common, so if a child confides in you, take him or her seriously. Don't turn a blind eye!"*
http://www.helpguide.org/articles/abuse/child-abuse-and-neglect.htm

There are a number of resources that can be accessed:

**Here is help for Childhood Sexual Abuse**

**1-888-PREVENT** (1-888-773-8368) – Stop It Now

**1-800-656-HOPE** – Rape, Abuse & Incest National Network (RAINN)

Statistics from RAINN- www.RAINN.ORG

Or visit ChiWorld.org for a list of other international child helplines.

The following are hotlines for Child Abuse:

- **US or Canada:** 1-800-422-4453 (Childhelp)
- **UK:** 0800 1111 (NSPCC Childline)
- **Australia:** 1800 688 009 (CAPS)
- **New Zealand:** 0800-543-754 (Kidsline)
- **Other international helplines:** Child Helpline International

I wish that we had had the courage of this young girl in a recent article I found: http://www.newslinq.com/mom-goes-ballistic/

Brené Brown: Rising Strong: The Reckoning, The Rumble and The Revolution © Penguin Random House LLC

Marianne Williamson: A Return to Love: Reflections on the Principles of "A Course in Miracles"

Icarus X., Phoenix: My Attempt to Rise from the Ashes of Childhood Abuse

Louise Hay: http://www.healyourlife.com/love-your-inner-child

Maureen Brady:  Beyond Survival: A Writing Journey for Healing Childhood Sexual Abuse

Caroline Myss: Defy Gravity: Healing Beyond the Bounds of Reason

http://www.theatlantic.com/national/archive/2013/01/america-has-an-incest-problem/272459/

https://en.wikipedia.org/wiki/Conscription

Just Another Number:  Maggie Young

Ellen Bass: The Courage to Heal: A Guide for Women Survivors of Child Sexual Abuse

Jeanne McElvaney: Childhood Abuse: Tips to Change Child Abuse Effects

http://www.dabs.uk.com/information/childhood-sexual-abuse-incest

A.B. Curtiss: "Brain Switch Out of Depression: Break the Cycle of Despair."

Lissa Rankin MD:  Mind Over Medicine: Scientific Proof You Can Heal Yourself (*Hay House, 2013*)

Yann Martel: Life of Pi

Margaret Atwood: Alias Grace

Jeanne McElvaney: Spirit Unbroken: Abby's Story